21

THINGS

YOU MAY NOT KNOW

ABOUT

THE INDIAN ACT

 BOB JOSEPH

INDIGENOUS
RELATIONS
PRESS

Indigenous Relations Press
www.ictinc.ca
Port Coquitlam BC

ISBN 978-0-9952665-2-0 (paperback)
ISBN 978-0-9952665-9-9 (ebook)

Produced by Page Two
www.pagetwostrategies.com
Design by Peter Cocking

PRAISE FOR
21 Things You May Not Know About the Indian Act

"I have a deep hope for Canada that there can be reconciliation. I want every Canadian to imagine a Canada in which every person will live with dignity, value, and purpose. But to do that, there must be reflection on our shared history and the harmful periods and events that continue to haunt us as a nation. Understanding the *Indian Act* is fundamental to understanding why those harmful periods and events took place. Bob Joseph's book is an invaluable tool for Canadians who want to understand the past in order to contribute to reconciliation in our country."

Chief Dr. Robert Joseph, *OBC*,
Ambassador, Reconciliation Canada

"From declaring cultural ceremonies illegal to prohibiting pool hall owners from granting Indigenous Peoples entrance, from forbidding the speaking of Indigenous languages to the devastating policy that created residential schools, Bob Joseph reveals the hold this paternalistic act, with its roots in the 1800s, still has on the lives of Indigenous Peoples in Canada in the twenty-first century. This straightforward book is an invaluable resource. There is much for non-Indigenous people to learn and to do. But equally important, there is much to unlearn and to undo. The time is right for this book. Thank you, Bob Joseph. Gilakas'la."

Shelagh Rogers, *OC*, *Truth and Reconciliation Commission of Canada Honorary Witness*

"Increasing Canadians' knowledge about the terrible foundation this country has been built on is a critical part of reconciliation. Bob Joseph has highlighted some of the unbelievable provisions of the *Indian Act* and how they have impacted First Nations in Canada, and gives a brief overview of what we may replace it with going forward. His book provides helpful context to the dialogue that needs to take place in Canada."

Kim Baird, *OC, OBC, Owner, Kim Baird Strategic Consulting; Member of the Tsawwassen First Nation and Negotiator of the Tsawwassen First Nation Treaty*

"Bob Joseph, one of the pre-eminent instructors in Canada on how to develop positive relations with Indigenous Peoples, has written a must-read book for business leaders. His straightforward writing style paints a picture so that all Canadians can appreciate the draconian and oppressive nature of the country's most racist legislation. The book identifies restrictions that range from laughable—prohibiting First Nations Peoples from entering pool halls—to sinister—forbidding First Nations Peoples from practising their traditional beliefs and speaking their language. If you want to work with First Nations communities, read this book."

Clint Davis, *Partner and Managing Director,*
ACASTA CAPITAL INDIGENOUS

"Bob Joseph provides an incredible glimpse into the lengths the Canadian government took to limit Indigenous Peoples from achieving health, wealth, and cultural connections through the *Indian Act*. That much of this is still legal today is baffling, as he provides examples of how assimilation at all costs is still the end goal of the *Indian Act*. Canada still has much work to do to achieve reconciliation with Indigenous Peoples and, as Bob says, 'to dismantle the *Indian Act* once and for all.'"

Ginger Gosnell-Myers,
Manager, Aboriginal Relations, City of Vancouver

"Bob Joseph's ability to navigate the complex history of the *Indian Act* is a wonder to behold. He provides depth and knowledge for Indigenous and non-Indigenous scholars alike. His articulate, insightful and comprehensive analysis on the history of the *Indian Act* provides a sound understanding of the present narrative of Indigenous Peoples in Canada. This book provides an excellent analysis of the ongoing relationship and predicament between provincial and federal governments and Indigenous Peoples in the twenty-first century."

J.P. Gladu, *President and CEO,*
Canadian Council for Aboriginal Business

"though they killed us
... we live
they put us down
yet we stand
they deny
but there is truth"

guujaaw

~~~~~~

**HELPING CANADIANS
MAKE RECONCILIATION WITH
INDIGENOUS PEOPLES
A REALITY**

‖‖

TO CANADA AND RECONCILIATION

_____

When the present does not recognize the wrongs of the past, the future takes its revenge. For that reason, we must never, never turn away from the opportunity of confronting history together—the opportunity to right a historical wrong.

GOVERNOR GENERAL MICHAËLLE JEAN
at relaunch of the Truth and Reconciliation
Commission of Canada, October 2009

It is readily acknowledged that Indian children lose their natural resistance to illness by habituating so closely in the residential schools and that they die at a much higher rate than in their villages. But this alone does not justify a change in the policy of the Department, which is geared towards a final solution of our Indian Problem.

DUNCAN CAMPBELL SCOTT,
Deputy Superintendent of Indian Affairs, 1910

Contents

IIIIIIIIIIIIIIIIIIIIIIIIIIIIIIIIIIIIIII

Acknowledgements

IN WORKING ON this book I learned that as the author, I had the easiest job. Transforming a manuscript on Google Docs into a book and getting it into bookstores was beyond my ability. It was my great good fortune to discover the team at Page Two Strategies Inc. The publishing process is both fascinating and slightly intimidating, but the professionals at Page Two guided me through the stages and kept the intimidating aspect at a low murmur. Trena White, principal, instantly grasped why this book had to be available to all Canadians. Her excitement was uplifting and affirming. Amanda Lewis, project and development manager, poured her expertise into keeping the book development on course and on time. Working with Peter Cocking on cover and interior design was enthralling and an honour. Zoe Grams, marketing, was an endless source of energy and innovative marketing ideas and strategies. I would also like to thank Julie Domvile for her encouragement that this book was a necessary component of reconciliation, and for all her work on the research required to flesh out the punitive policies and prohibitions of the *Indian Act*.

To my many family and friends who have shared their knowledge along the way, thank you.

This book would not have happened if my way better half, Cindy Joseph, had not supported me in seeing the nugget of an idea transform into a book.

Deep gratitude to every Canadian who reads this book and takes to heart a commitment of reconciliation.

Introduction

〜〜〜〜〜〜〜〜〜〜〜〜〜〜〜〜〜〜〜〜〜〜〜〜〜〜〜〜〜〜〜〜〜

AS A BLOGGER and trainer on Indigenous topics, in 2015 I decided to write an article about the *Indian Act*. My goal was to simply provide some "take-aways" about the Act for our learners and our blog *Working Effectively with Indigenous Peoples®*. Of the Act's many aggressive, destructive, and frequently contradictory statutes and policies, I selected 21 that were not common knowledge and called the article "21 Things You Might Not Have Known About the Indian Act." Response to the article was immense, intense, and enduring. The first month alone we had over 55,000 visitors to our website just from Facebook.

This response showed there was a real lack of information about First Nations (Indians) and non–First Nations but, more importantly, a real interest in learning about the *Indian Act* and its impacts. It made me realize the significance of the information and how knowing about the *Indian Act* could help people understand how it shaped the socio-economic and political reality of many generations of First Nations, and how it is the basis for many of today's stereotypes about First Nations. In reality, there was a foregone conclusion that Indians would simply die out, cease to exist, thereby absolving the government of any financial responsibility and giving clear access to the lands reserved for Indians.

I think it is critical that non-Indigenous Canadians be aware of how deeply the *Indian Act* penetrated, controlled, and continues to control, most aspects of the lives of First Nations. It is an instrument of oppression. If true reconciliation between Indigenous Peoples, the federal government, and non-Indigenous Canadians is going to be achieved, an understanding of how the *Indian Act*—despite its many amendments and modifications—continues to direct the lives of First Nations and constrains the opportunities for First Nations and Canadians alike is essential.

IN MY PROFESSIONAL life as an Indigenous relations trainer I am aware of the gap in knowledge regarding the history of Indigenous Peoples that spans from Confederation in 1867 to the 1960s. In my professional life I am also heartened by the increasing number of Canadians who register for my training because they want to learn and understand.

IN MY PERSONAL life as an Indigenous person I look for opportunities to build bridges of reconciliation by providing information about Indigenous Peoples. My personal quest is to change the world, one person at a time. The continued interest in the article indicated to me that a book expanding the 21 things would provide a service to Canadians, and others, who are ready to learn about the *Indian Act* and its ramifications. This book is for people who want to walk with informed minds and hearts along the path to reconciliation.

It is time to dismantle the *Indian Act* once and for all—no further amendments, no more bandaging or tweaking of the Act. It will not be easy, but it can be done. In fact, it has been done by the Nisga'a Nation. They are self-determining, self-governing, and, most importantly, self-reliant.

Some might say that getting rid of the Act will be like moving out of the frying pan and into the fire, as though this is a bad thing. But I don't agree. We can also think about fire as a new opportunity. In Kwak'wala we have the term "i'tusto," which means "to rise again." Getting rid of the *Indian Act* will give First Nations, and Canada the nation state, the opportunity to rise again to be better and to be stronger.

I hope you will join me in this quest to change the world one person at a time. I know that this book can contribute to that goal.

GILAKAS'LA
BOB JOSEPH

The Indian Act

||||||||||||||||||||||||||||||||||||||||||||||||||||||||||||||||||||||||

THE ROOTS OF the *Indian Act* lie in the *Bagot Report*
of 1844 that recommended that control over Indian matters be centralized, that the children be sent to boarding
schools away from the influence of their communities
and culture, that the Indians be encouraged to assume
the European concept of free enterprise, and that land be
individually owned under an Indian land registry system
in which they could sell to each other but not to non-
Indians. The *Bagot Report* provided the framework for the
Indian Act, 1876.

When the *British North America Act* (BNA), or what is
now known as the *Constitution Act, 1867* was issued, it
gave, under Section 91(24), exclusive jurisdiction over
"Indians and lands reserved for the Indians" to the federal
government. With issue of the BNA, Canada was placed
in a position of conflict of interest. On the one hand it was
responsible for "Indians and lands reserved for Indians,"
while, on the other hand, it was the responsible party
for negotiating treaties and purchasing their land for the
Crown.

Eight years later, when the regulations that impacted
Indians were consolidated into the *Indian Act, 1876*, we
start to get some insight into Indian policy:

> Our Indian legislation generally rests on the principle, that the aborigines are to be kept in a condition of tutelage and treated as wards or children of the State ... [T]he true interests of the aborigines and of the State alike require that every effort should be made to aid the Red man in lifting himself out of his condition of tutelage and dependence, and that is clearly our wisdom and our duty, through education and every other means, to prepare him for a higher civilization by encouraging him to assume the privileges and responsibilities of full citizenship.[1]

But that paternalistic attitude gave way to increasingly punitive rules, prohibitions, and regulations that dehumanized Indians. By the 1920s, Indian policy took on a much darker tone. Duncan Campbell Scott, the Deputy Superintendent General of Indian Affairs, wrote: "I want to get rid of the Indian problem... Our objective is to continue until there is not an Indian that has not been absorbed into the body politic, and there is no Indian question, and no Indian Department..."[2]

When details about the atrocities of World War II became known, coupled with the contributions by Indigenous soldiers during the war, Canadians began to judge how the government treated Indians. Information about the staggering number of deaths of children in residential schools began to creep out. Mainstream Canada took notice. To counter the negativity, the federal government commissioned a series of positive, short films about the schools, one of which signs off with "for the oldest Canadians, a new future."[3] There was a call for a Royal

Commission to investigate Indian Affairs, the conditions on reserves, and discrimination against Indians. While the Royal Commission never took shape, a Special Joint Parliamentary Committee of the Senate and the House of Commons was formed to look into Canada's policies and the management of Indian Affairs. After two years of hearings, the Joint Committee recommended:

a) The complete revision or repeal of every section in the Indian Act.

b) That Canada's Indian Act be designed to make possible the gradual transition of the Indian from a position of wardship to citizenship. To achieve this goal the act should provide that:
   i   Indian women be given a political voice in band affairs.
   ii Bands should be allowed more self-government.
   iii Bands should be given more financial assistance.
   iv Indians should be treated the same as non-Indians in the matter of intoxicants.
   v   Indian Affairs officials were to have their duties and responsibilities designed so as to assist the Indians attain the full rights of citizenship and to serve the responsibilities of self-government.
   vi Bands be allowed to incorporate as municipalities.

c) The guidelines for future policy were to be:
   i   The easing of enfranchisement procedures.
   ii Indians should be given the vote.
   iii When possible co-operate with the provinces in delivering services to the Indian people.

iv Indian education should be geared for assimilation; therefore it should take place with non-Indian students.[4]

Despite the recommendations, a 1951 amendment to the Act did not in fact bring much in the way of relief to Indians from the government's formidable control over most aspects of their lives. This book deals primarily with the Indian Act and its many reiterations between 1869 and 1951. The *Indian Act* remains in effect today, with basically the same framework it had in 1876, despite the numerous amendments.

In this book I have endeavoured to provide insight into just 21 of the rules, regulations, and prohibitions of the *Indian Act*. It is an incredibly broad topic and a vast body of law that, in its entirety, continues to touch on every aspect of an Indian person's life, from the womb to the tomb. Had I written about the entire *Indian Act*, it is unlikely anyone would read the book and we would have fallen down in our mission to inform people so that they can understand the past and move towards reconciliation. If you are interested in reading the full text of the *Indian Act, 1876*, please visit https://www.aadnc-aandc.gc.ca/DAM/DAM-INTER-HQ/STAGING/texte-text/1876c18_1100100010253_eng.pdf.

NOTE ON TERMINOLOGY

I use the word "Indian" in the first two sections of the book because of its legal and historical context. It is not a term we would otherwise use unless in reference to a community that has made that choice for their name. One example of this is the Musqueam Indian Band.

"Indian" in the context of the *Indian Act* is a status Indian. One of the many actions of the Act was the definition of a segment of society based on genetics. Over the evolution of the *Indian Act*, a great deal of attention was devoted to who would be classified as an Indian and who would not. Many amendments, such as those involving enfranchisement and women, were designed with the goal of reducing the number of people who identified as status Indians.

So, how was an "Indian" defined?

In the 1876 *Indian Act*, the term "Indian" meant

- any male person of Indian blood reported to belong to a particular band
- any child of such a person
- any woman who is or was lawfully married to such a person

That definition changed in the 1951 revision of the *Indian Act* to

- a person who pursuant to the Act is registered as an Indian

A status Indian (registered Indian) has legal rights to benefits and restrictions offered by federal agencies and provincial governments. Usage of "Indian" will continue as long as there is an *Indian Act.*

In the 1970s the term "First Nation" came into usage as the replacement for the term "Indian band." Many communities made the move to use "First Nation" rather than "band" in their name. "First Nation" can refer to a single band or, in the plural form, many bands. Indians are also known as "First Nations," and in the third part of this book we switch to that term as that was the term used in that era.

In some instances we use the term "Indigenous Peoples" to replace the term "Indians," as that's the term that is, at this time, being used more commonly than "First Nation." "Indigenous Peoples" is also the collective term for First Nation, Inuit, and Métis Peoples who live in Canada.

In 2016, the federal government replaced "Aboriginal" with "Indigenous" in government communications. This may not seem like a particularly big deal but it is, as by doing so, the government took a giant step back to the nation-to-nation relationship established in 1763 when the Royal Proclamation[5] was signed by King George III. This is a momentous change that reflects the relationship between Indigenous Peoples in Canada and non-Indigenous people.

We use the term "Aboriginal Peoples" to indicate the collective group of people who hold various rights and obligations under provisions of the *Indian Act* and Section 35 of the *Constitution Act, 1982*. Additionally, we use it in reference the names of reports and publications.

Yes, I agree, it's all very confusing and will continue to be so for some time yet as the Canadian government sorts through its relationship with Indigenous Peoples. But hang in there!

DARK CHAPTER

The Beginning

||||||||||||||||||||||||||||||||||||||||||||||||||||||||||||||||||||||||

... to wean them by slow degrees, from their nomadic habits, which have almost become an instinct, and by slow degrees absorb them or settle them on the land. Meantime, they must be fairly protected.

JOHN A. MACDONALD, *1880*[1]

1 Imposed the elected chief and band council system
1869[2] TO PRESENT DAY

The *Indian Act* election system, in which the majority of our First Nation members still operate, has severely impacted the manner in which our societies traditionally governed themselves. It has displaced or attempted to displace our inherent authority as leaders and has eroded our traditions, culture, and belief systems. It does not reflect our needs and aspirations. It has also not kept pace with principles of modern and accountable governments.

LAWRENCE PAUL, *Co-Chair, Atlantic Policy Congress of First Nations Chiefs Secretariat, 2009*[3]

Long before European contact, Indigenous nations had effectively and sustainably governed themselves. Each nation had its own distinctive political institution, traditions, leadership system, economy, culture, and economy, and had autonomous control over its territories and resources within.

European-style elections for chief and council were introduced to Indigenous communities in 1869 under *An Act for the Gradual Enfranchisement of Indians, the Better Management of Indian Affairs, and to Extend the Provisions of the Act*. The imposed system was and still is similar to municipal-style government in which a leader and council members are elected, based on the terms and conditions of the government. The role of the elected chief is to administer the *Indian Act*, and in no meaningful way does this reflect their former self-government.

The dismissal of Indigenous forms of government in favour of the European-style municipal government displaced traditional political structures and did not reflect, consider, or honour Indigenous needs and values. A chief was more likely to be elected based on his ability to communicate and negotiate with government agencies as well as maintain his commitment to community, values, and traditions. The federal government also did not recognize that each Nation had its own style of governance with specialized skills, tools, authority, and capacity developed over centuries. Imposing European-style elections was designed for assimilation—to remake traditional cultures in the image of the colonizers.

The impetus behind imposing a new elective system was to replace what the federal government viewed as an "irresponsible" system with a responsible system. This new elective system was "designed to pave the way to the establishment of simple municipal institutions."[4] In other words, traditional band and tribal government were considered an impediment to the federal government's plans for advancement.

William Spragge, Deputy Superintendent of Indian Affairs, in the 1870s is said to have observed that Indian opposition to adopting what was clearly an alien election system was not because of its cultural inappropriateness, but because "the Indian mind is in general slow to accept improvements." He stated, "it would be premature to conclude that the bands are averse to the elective principle, because they are backward in perceiving the privileges which it confers."[5] The arrogance of the federal government in assuming that existing systems were "irresponsible" blindfolded them to existing wise, inclusive, and foundational Indigenous governance systems.

Initially, it was stipulated that elections were to be held on an annual basis. Then in 1898 it was changed to every three years, and in the 1951 *Indian Act* it was changed to every two years, which is how it remains today for most bands. The Department of Indian Affairs, not the people who elected the chief, held the power to depose a chief. Only males over the age of 23 were allowed to vote and Indian women were not given the right to vote in band elections until the 1951 *Indian Act*.

Control of many elements of the reserve, including land, resources, and finance, were passed into the hands of the Department of Indian Affairs as Indigenous Peoples were considered unsophisticated and incapable of managing their own affairs. The chiefs were granted little in the way of bylaw powers, and those limited powers were not at all reflective of their former self-governing powers, which further emasculated them and their role in leading their nation. Their role was (and is) to administer the *Indian Act*.

Here's a list of what chiefs' decision-making powers were reduced to:

1. The care of the public health;
2. The observance of order and decorum at assemblies of the Indians in general council, or on other occasions;
3. The repression of intemperance and profligacy;
4. The prevention of trespass by cattle;
5. The maintenance of roads, bridges, ditches and fences;
6. The construction and repair of school houses, council houses and other Indian public buildings;
7. The establishment of pounds and the appointment of pound-keepers;
8. The locating of the land in their reserves, and the establishment of a register of such locations.[6]

The two-year election cycle exacerbated the inability of chiefs and councils to make any significant progress on long-term development initiatives, govern and act in the best interests of their citizens, or build effective foundations for community development.

The potential for leadership changes every two years can make it difficult for economic development projects to progress, especially certain resource development projects that are decades in the planning phase. Political instability and economic development are not good bedfellows. The two-year election cycle also makes it difficult for tribal groups to work together on larger initiatives because elections are all held at different times. Different chiefs, who may not be up to speed on an initiative or who may have a different vision, join the group at different times, which can impede the progress of the initiative.

Another impact of the imposed European-style elections and short term of office is the unending cycle of divisiveness that elections foster within communities. The constant manoeuvring and strategizing for power in the next election pits community members, and frequently family members, against one another. The cohesive, traditional belief that rights are collectively held tends to get lost in the quest to win an election. Not all elected chiefs share the same priorities for how resources should be distributed within the community.

As the goal of the elected band council system was to undermine traditional governance and augment assimilation, many Indigenous people refuse to vote in band elections. Additionally, many refuse to vote in federal elections, although that trend is slowly changing and Indigenous individuals are increasingly running for office in municipal, provincial, and federal elections.

2 Denied women status

1869 TO 1985

Provided always that any Indian woman marrying any other than an Indian, shall cease to be an Indian within the meaning of this Act, nor shall the children issue of such marriage be considered as Indians within the

meaning of this Act; Provided also, that any Indian
woman marrying an Indian of any other tribe, band
or body shall cease to be a member of the tribe, band
or body to which she formerly belonged, and become
a member of the tribe, band or body of which her
husband is a member, and the children, issue of this
marriage, shall belong to their father's tribe only.

An Act for the Gradual Enfranchisement of Indians, 1869[7]

Prior to European contact, and the ensuing fundamental disruption to the traditional lifestyle of Indigenous communities, women were central to the family. They were revered in the communities that identified as matriarchal societies, had roles within community government and spiritual ceremonies, and were generally respected for the sacred gifts bestowed upon them by the Creator.

In 1742, Joseph-François Lafitau, a French Jesuit missionary and ethnologist, wrote about his observations of the role of women in the Iroquois-speaking nations:

Nothing is more real, however, than the women's superiority. It is they who really maintain the tribe... In them resides all the real authority: the lands, the fields, and all their harvest belong to them; they are the soul of the councils, the arbiter of peace and war... they arrange the marriages; the children are under their authority; and the order of succession is founded in their blood.[8]

The *Indian Act* disrespected, ignored, and undermined the role of women in many ways. This dissolution of women's stature, coupled with the abuses of the residential school system, has been a significant contributor to the vulnerability of Indigenous women.

The *Indian Act* subjected generations of Indigenous women and their children to a legacy of discrimination when it was first enacted in 1867, and it continues to do so today despite amendments. *Indian Act* policies made women unequal to Indian men (who did not lose status when they married non-Indian women) and to non-Indian women (who acquired Indian status by marrying Indian men). Not all, but many, women have faced difficulty in being recognized as both Indians and women in Canada.

Federal law in the late 1800s defined a status Indian solely on the basis of paternal lineage—an Indian was a male Indian, the wife of a male Indian, or the child of a male Indian. Despite amendments, federal law continues to be a quagmire that discriminates against, dishonours, and disrespects Indigenous women.

Under Section 12 of the 1951 *Indian Act*, an Indian woman who married a non-Indian man was not entitled to be registered, and thus lost her status. Section 12 also removed status from a woman whose mother and paternal grandmother had not been status Indians before their marriages. These women could be registered, but they lost their Indian status as soon as they turned 21.

Indian men, however, did not lose their status when they married non-Indian women. Between 1958 and 1968 alone, more than 100,000 women and children lost their Indian status as a result of these provisions.[9]

In 1985, the *Indian Act* was amended by the passage of Bill C-31 to remove discrimination against women, to be consistent with Section 15 of the Canadian Charter of Rights and Freedoms,[10] but gender discrimination remains. For example, in some families Indian women who lost status through marrying out before 1985 can pass Indian status on to their children but not to their children's children. This is known as the "second generation cut-off." However, their brothers, who may also have married out before 1985, can pass on status to their children for at least one more generation, even though the children of the sister and the brother all have one status Indian parent and one non-Indian parent.[11]

Amendments to Bill C-31 provided a process by which women could apply for reinstatement of their lost Indian status. While such an amendment looks good on paper, in some cases it proved to be extremely difficult for women to actually execute the process. The first of many hurdles for women was navigating the Department of Indian and Northern Affairs' (DIAND) complex documentation system. The numerous requests for additional information combined with the DIAND's significant underestimation of the sheer volume of applicants and its inability to process the applications due to inadequate staffing levels frequently left the applicants in prolonged states of limbo. Besides the daunting magnitude of red tape involved, a more heartless aspect of the reinstatement process was the cost applicants were forced to bear. Many women had to travel from sometimes very remote communities to centres that had DIAND offices. The research and documentation fees and travel requirements simply put the dream of reinstatement, which opened the door to better health and education services for the women and their children, out of reach for many women who were already financially marginalized due to their lack of "status." The *Report of the Royal Commission on Aboriginal Peoples* noted in 1996 that the amendments to Bill C-31 affected all bands in Canada but did little to change the discrimination against women in the *Indian Act*.

Introduced in March 2010, Bill C-3 was supposed to be the remedy, but it actually continued the discrimination. Grandchildren born before September 4, 1951, who trace their Indigenous heritage through their maternal parentage are still denied status, while those who trace their heritage through their paternal counterparts are not.

Indian Act regulations devalue women and are considered the primary cause of the vulnerability of Indigenous women today. The Native Women's Association of Canada states, "These systemic issues have directly caused poor health and mental health, economic insecurity, homelessness, lack of justice, addictions and low educational attainment for Aboriginal women and girls, placing them in precarious situations where the risk for violence is greater."[12]

Peggy J. Blair writes about the rights of Indigenous women on- and off-reserve:

> Aboriginal women are more likely to face domestic abuse than other women in Canada. While one in ten women in Canada is abused by her partner, almost one in three Aboriginal women is abused. If an Aboriginal woman leaves the reserve to escape domestic abuse, she can lose her home. There are long waiting lists for housing on-reserve and often a great deal of pressure on band councils to re-allocate housing as soon as possible. Many Aboriginal women who wish to live on-reserve cannot do so, because of a lack of housing... At present, Indian women do not have the same human rights or protection of their rights as Canadian women.[13]

3 Created reserves
1876 TO PRESENT DAY

Reserves were regarded for much of the 19th century as places for Indians to be confined until they became "civilized." Once they had learned "proper habits" of industry and thrift, they could then be released (enfranchised, in the language of Indian legislation from this period) into the general society as full citizens with equal rights and responsibilities, taking with them a proportional share of reserve assets.

A reserve is a tract of land set aside under the *Indian Act* and treaty agreements for the exclusive use of an Indian band. At least that's how a reserve is described on paper. In reality, reserves were created as a means of containing and controlling Indians while providing European settlers full access to the fish and game, water, timber, and mineral resources that had formerly sustained Indian life and culture.

Early examples of reserves date back to attempts by French missionaries in 1637 to encourage Indians to settle in one spot and embrace both agriculture and Christianity. The settlers wanted to establish farms and communities and began cutting timber to open up the land for agriculture and availing themselves of fish and game. It became apparent to the authorities that an effective means was needed to ensure the most fertile land and access to resources was available to European farmers.

Two of the goals of the government under John A. Macdonald were to lure European settlers to Canadian soil and to build a railway linking the west coast with Ottawa. The government needed access to the land for settlement and development. Standing in the government's way were hundreds of Indigenous communities comprised of thousands of people living their traditional lives on their traditional lands. Reserves met the government's need to contain and relocate communities that stood in the way of making room for settlers. In a letter to Adams George Archibald, the Lieutenant-Governor of Manitoba, on November 18, 1870, Prime Minister John A. Macdonald wrote:

> Sir, We are looking anxiously for your report as to Indian titles both within Manitoba and without; and as to the best means of extinguishing [terminating] the Indian titles in the valley of Saskatchewan. Would you kindly give us your views on that point, officially and unofficially? We should take immediate steps to extinguish the Indian titles somewhere in the Fertile Belt in the valley of Saskatchewan, and open it for settlement. There will otherwise be an influx of squatters who will seize upon the most eligible positions and greatly disturb the symmetry [organization] of future surveys.[14]

Reserves were either a portion of Indigenous Peoples' traditional land or they were tracts of land far away from their traditional lands. There wasn't a consistent formula for designating land to a band. For example, Treaties 1 and 2 used the ratio of 160 acres per family of five; Treaties 3 to 11 allocated 640 acres per family of five. In British Columbia, the ratio was an average of 20 acres granted per family.

Moses Smith of the Nuu-chah-nulth Nation in Port Alberni, BC, expressed his frustration with the reserve system to the Royal Commission on Aboriginal People:

> We got absolutely the short end of the stick. And to
> quote what was said, what was said of us, we, as Nuu-
> chah-nulth people, "These people, they don't need the
> land. They make their livelihood from the sea."... So,
> here we have just mere little rock piles on the west
> coast of Vancouver Island, the territory of the Nuu-
> chah-nulth Nation. Rock piles! Rock piles![15]

The reality for the bands under the reserve system was they lost land, which constricted their ability to hunt, trap, fish, and harvest traditional foods to sustain themselves. The scarcity of traditional foods combined with the introduction of foreign foodstuffs, the change in lifestyle, and exposure to European viruses and diseases caused Indians' immune systems to weaken and made them more vulnerable to malnourishment and disease.

Indigenous people were also forced into European-style homes that were inappropriate for the traditional concept of family and often inappropriate for the climate. Traditional dwellings were contingent on the environment and on food-gathering or hunting traditions. The European, single family–style housing was counter to the tradition of community collectivity of many Indigenous cultures in which a number of families lived together with open space for meeting, eating, and practising spirituality. It must be understood that the houses are owned by the federal government, not the people who live in them.

Some communities were removed altogether from their traditional lands, breaking their connection to the land that was part of their history, culture, and identity. In other words, all they had known all their lives was gone and they were left facing a future impoverished, malnour-ished, vulnerable to disease, and controlled by the Crown.

4 Encouraged voluntary and enforced enfranchisement
1876 TO 1985

The ultimate purpose of enfranchisement (loss of status rights) was to encourage assimilation and to reduce the number of Indians the federal government was financially responsible for—to get "rid of the Indian problem." It needs to be recognized that "status Indians" were not con-sidered "people" according to Canadian laws and did not become "people" until the *Indian Act* was revised in 1951.

Prior to 1951, the *Indian Act* defined a "person" as "an individual other than an Indian." An Indigenous person's only avenue to being recognized as a "person" was to give up their Indian status, which was known as voluntary enfranchisement. Once they were "people" they assumed all the rights other Canadians enjoyed, but it also meant they gave up associated legal rights, benefits, and restric-tions of being a status Indian. A less apparent objective of enfranchisement was to break up reserve land, undermine the collective worldview of the people, and promote the adoption of a European worldview of individual rights. It had the potential to be a slow dismemberment of land and culture.

Indian men over the age of 21 who were deemed sober and industrious could apply for enfranchisement. If they qualified, they would receive an allotment of land carved from their home reserve; after three years, they would receive a title deed to the land. If they died without heirs, the allotment would be turned over to the Crown. If the man was married, his wife and children were automatically enfranchised, and if he died and left children under the age of 21, they would become wards of the government.

To become a British subject—to shed the confines of the *Indian Act*, embrace full rights of colonial citizenship, and become "civilized"—was considered a privilege by the government. They expected Indians would be eager to apply for enfranchisement, but they were sorely mistaken; only one man voluntarily took up the offer. Band leaders were deeply disturbed by the *Gradual Civilization Act* and not supportive of their young men turning their backs on their heritage and traditions and taking a piece of land from the collective. This poignant letter from the Oneida Indians of Muney Town and other Bands on the River Thames to the Governor General in 1858 sums it up:

> It is with feelings of sorrow that we hear of the act passed for the purpose of allowing the Indian to enfranchise if he feels desirous of doing so, we are sorry that such an inducement is held out to separate our people. If any person availing himself of this enfranchisement act should fail to do well and lose his little piece of ground—he is forbidden to ever return to his tribe. All red men are brethren and our hearts would bleed to see one of our brethren wandering about the highway without the right of returning to his tribe when in distress.[16]

Indian leaders and communities vehemently opposed the *Gradual Civilization Act*, petitioned for its appeal, refused to take part in the annual band census, and refused to allow surveyors on their reserves to mark out the incentive allotments. Up until this Act was passed, relations between band councils and government representatives had been relatively co-operative. The nation-to-nation relationship as outlined in the Royal Proclamation of 1763 was gone and in its place was a relationship of acrimony and deep distrust. Passage of this Act showed a Crown that had turned its back on the Proclamation's decree that the reserve land base be protected—it marked a profound shift in relations between the Crown and Indians.

When it became apparent that Indians were not taking up enfranchisement as expected, the government ramped up its efforts with the 1880 amendment to the *Indian Act*, which required compulsory enfranchisement for anyone who obtained a degree or became a clergyman:

> Any Indian who may be admitted to the degree of Doctor of Medicine, or to any other degree by any University of Learning, or who may be admitted in any Province of the Dominion to practice law either as an Advocate or as a Barrister or Counsellor, or Solicitor or Attorney or to be a Notary Public, or who may enter Holy Orders, or who may be licensed by any denomination of Christians as a Minister of the Gospel, may upon petition to the Superintendent-General, *ipso facto* become and be enfranchised under the provisions of this Act; and the Superintendent-General may give him a suitable allotment of land from the lands belonging to the band of which he is a member.[17]

In 1920, the *Indian Act* was amended and compulsory enfranchisement was again included. The "fitness" of an Indian (male or female) over the age of 21 to become enfranchised was to be decided by a board of examiners. Following their assessment, the Indian would be enfranchised two years later. This provision was repealed two years later, only to be reintroduced in a modified form in 1933, where it remained until revision of the *Indian Act* in 1951.

At this time an additional modification was made that saw the compulsory enfranchisement of Indian women who married non-Indian men; this modification remained in the Act until 1985.

Later, enfranchisement was extended to include Indians who joined the military. Indian veterans returning from World War II found that while they may have fought for their country, they had lost their Indian status in the process and had no home to return to.

The right to vote was also tied to enfranchisement until 1960, when Indians were deemed worthy of being able to vote in federal elections. Please see #20, "Denied Indians the right to vote."

{ 2 }

Resistance Is Futile

IIIIIIIIIIIIIIIIIIIIIIIIIIIIIIIIIIIIIIIIIIIIIIIIIIIIIIIIIIIIIIIIIIIIIIIIIIIIIIIIIIIIIIII

... we have been pampering and coaxing the Indians;
that we must take a new course, we must vindicate the
position of the white man, we must teach the Indians
what law is, we must not pauperize them, as they say
we have been doing.

JOHN A. MACDONALD, *1885*[1]

5   Could expropriate portions of reserves for public works
1876 TO CURRENT VERSION OF INDIAN ACT, 1985

Land. If you understand nothing else about the history of
Indians in North America, you need to understand that
the question that really matters is the question of land.

THOMAS KING, *The Inconvenient Indian: A Curious
Account of Native People in North America, 2012*[2]

The 1876 *Indian Act* outlined its policy about land:

If any railway, road, or public work passes through or
causes injury to any reserve belonging to or in possession

of any band of Indians, or if any act occasioning damage to any reserve be done under the authority of any Act of Parliament, or of the legislature of any province, compensation shall be made to them therefor in the same manner as is provided with respect to the lands or rights of other persons; the Superintendent-General shall in any case in which an arbitration may be had, name the arbitrator on behalf of the Indians, and shall act for them in any matter relating to the settlement of such compensation; and the amount awarded in any case shall be paid to the Receiver General for the use of the band of Indians for whose benefit the reserve is held, and for the benefit of any Indian having improvements thereon.[3]

The *Indian Act, 1876* took for granted that Indians' land could be expropriated by any private group or level of government wanting a way through it. Ten years later, expropriation for such purposes required government consent, and it was still the government that negotiated settlements on Indians' behalf.[4] It would not be long before the government could also remove an Indian band from a reserve deemed too close to a town or city of 8,000 or more. The Kitsilano Reserve, located under the south side of the Burrard Bridge in Vancouver, BC, is an example of this:

1869 37 acres are set aside at the mouth of False Creek for Indian people.

1877 The reserve is expanded to 80 acres, allotted solely to the Squamish Nation people.

1901 A seven-acre right of way is obtained by Canadian Pacific Railway.

1904 Squamish Nation people surrender 11 acres for lease to a lumber company; agreement terms include jobs, lumber for houses, a protective fence around the cemetery, and compensation for loss of an orchard; some jobs in the mill are provided.

April 1911 It is discussed in Parliament that a reserve near a town is a hindrance to development.

May 1911 The *Indian Act* is amended, removing the need for band council approval: "Section 46 gave municipalities or companies the right to expropriate parts of reserves to build roads, railways, or other public facilities subject to the approval of the federal government. Section 49(a) was even more alarming to Native leaders: it gave the government the right to relocate any reserve situated near a town of eight thousand or more residents without having to obtain the prior approval of the reserve's residents."[5]

1913 Provincial representatives bypass the *Indian Act* and convince Squamish leaders to sell the land and leave; male heads of each family are given $11,250; their belongings are barged elsewhere and their houses are burnt; the land remains under the control of the *Indian Act*.

1916 The Harbour Commission expropriates the property for development, and holds it for a decade before abandoning its interest in it.

1930 Expropriation of reserve lands for public works allows the City of Vancouver to claim 6.2 acres of the reserve for the Burrard Street Bridge.

1934 The Department of National Defence applies for and is granted 4 acres.

1942 Indian Affairs leases 41.74 acres to the Department of Defence for the duration of World War II.

1947–1965 The reserve is broken into parcels and sold.

1977 The Squamish Nation launches legal efforts to reclaim portions of reserve; the Musqueam Indian Band and Tsleil-Waututh Nation launch counterclaims to interests in former reserve land.

2002 The Squamish Nation is victorious in reclaiming one small portion of its former reserve.[6]

This is one example of how the government manipulated the *Indian Act* to suit its needs.

6 Renamed individuals with European names
1880 TO UNDETERMINED TIME

(FOR THE PURPOSE OF REGISTERING INDIANS)

As early as 1850, the colonial government in British North America began to keep and maintain records to identify individual Indians and the bands to which they belonged. These records helped agents of the Crown to determine which people were eligible for treaty and interest benefits under specific treaties... In 1951, changes to the *Indian Act* included a change to create an Indian Register.

INDIGENOUS AND NORTHERN AFFAIRS CANADA,
"The Indian Register"[7]

The federal government's *Indian Act* policies during the 19th century were primarily concerned with assimilation. One aspect of the assimilation process was the renaming of the entire population for the purpose of registering Indians; this was partly to extinguish traditional ties and partly because Euro-Canadians found many of the names confusing and difficult to pronounce. Traditional names went against the government's assimilation objectives; the government feared that leaving Indigenous people with their traditional names would take away their motivation to assimilate.

Traditionally, Indians had neither a Christian name nor a surname. They had hereditary names, spirit names, family names, clan names, animal names, or nicknames. Hereditary names, in some cultures, are considered intangible wealth and carry great responsibility and certain rights. Hereditary names have been described as being analogous to royal titles such as Duke of Edinburgh. In many cultures, the birth name was just for that one stage of life, and additional names were given to mark milestones, acts of bravery, or feats of strength. None of the great heritage, symbolism, or tradition associated with names was recorded, recognized, or respected during the renaming process.

Traditional naming practices did not make sense to the Indian agents, who were charged with recording the names of all people living on reserves. The diversity of names and naming practices also made record keeping difficult. While there was not a uniform approach adopted by all Indian agents for the renaming process, generally the agents assigned each man a Christian name and, more often than not, a non-Indigenous surname. Women were given Christian names and assigned the surname of their fathers or husbands.

The Indian agents on the west coast of Canada often used biblical names from different religious denominations, repeating them as they worked their way through their jurisdiction, which explains the frequency of unrelated families that share common last names. Or they used their own names. As all agents were male, very few, if any, female names were used. As I have written in other publications, this is how the process would have unfolded: An Indian agent would ask me my name, I would say "k'acksum nakwala", and they would write down "Bob Joseph." Often I am asked if I am related to the Josephs from the Squamish First Nation, to which I usually reply, "No, but I'm sure we had the same Indian agent." Once the Indian agent wrote down my name, I became a status Indian because my name was on a band list.[8]

It's ironic that Indigenous Peoples in Canada have surnames that date back only a few generations. It is certainly not the case for ancestral names, which date back to creation.

7 Created a permit system to control Indians' ability to sell products from farms
1881 TO 2014

No Band or irregular Band of Indians, and no Indian of any Band or irregular Band in the North-West Territories may, without the consent in writing of the

Indian Agent for the locality, sell, barter, exchange, or give to any person or persons whomsoever, any grain, or root crops, or other produce grown on any Indian Reserve in the North-West Territories, or any part of such Reserve; and any such sale, barter, exchange or gift shall be absolutely null and void.

Order-in-Council, August 9, 1888[9]

Agriculture was one objective chosen as the path for Indians to follow to become "civilized." But many reserves were located in areas that were unsuitable for agriculture. Government agencies later used the low success rate of some Indian farmers as reason to reduce the size of reserves.

Indian agents and farm instructors worked with Indians to teach them how to farm, although growing crops such as corn or rice was not new to some cultures. In Saskatchewan, in particular, some of the Indian farmers were very successful and grew crops and produce that were as good as or better than that produced by the settlers, and were in a position to compete with the settlers on a commercial basis. Settlers objected, claiming the Indians were being mollycoddled and receiving unfair advantages. The government responded with the permit-to-sell system. Indian farmers were then placed in the position of requiring a permit to leave their reserve and a permit to sell farm products (see #11 "Restricted Indians from leaving their reserve without permission from an Indian Agent"). To solidify the effectiveness of the permit system, settlers were prohibited from purchasing goods and services from Indian farmers.

The government also took aim at Indian farmers working together. Many helped each other out during the labour-intensive periods of tilling and harvesting. They were unable to mortgage reserve land to raise money to purchase equipment, so they pooled their resources to purchase equipment. The government responded by requiring that the purchase of farm machinery be approved by a local Indian agent. This example from Saskatchewan shows the challenges Indians faced:

> At Duck Lake in 1891, six or seven Indians together purchased a self-binder with the approval of the farm instructor. The implement dealer had to acquire the consent of the agent, who was ordered by Inspector McGibbon to object to the sale. No sale or delivery took place.[10]

This pooling of labour and resources went against the grain of Indian policy that was designed to eradicate the culture of community and cohesiveness and enforce individualism and self-reliance. Forcing Indians conform to the European social standard of individuality was more important than them being economically successful.

Livestock, however, was overlooked in the original permit-to-sell system. Between 1886 and 1892, there was an increase in cattle ownership, which coincided with an increase in demand in England for Canadian beef. That all came to an end in 1892 when the government closed this economic loophole and expanded the permit-to-sell system to include livestock.

In the 1951 *Indian Act*, the permit system was extended so that it applied to all Indians, but its enforcement gradually disappeared, although it wasn't repealed until 2014, over the objections of some chiefs.

The chiefs' concern about the repeal of the permit sections was that if the government removed only sections of the Act, this would allow the Act to continue to exist into an undefined future. They argued that they didn't want temporary solutions but wanted real change away from the *Indian Act*, and sooner rather than later.

{ 3 }

Tightening Control

||||||||||||||||||||||||||||||||||||||||||||||||||||||||||||||||||||||||||||||||||||

The great aim of our legislation has been to do away with the tribal system and assimilate the Indian people in all respects with the other inhabitants of the Dominion as speedily as they are fit to change.

JOHN A. MACDONALD, *1885*[1]

8 Prohibited sale of ammunition to Indians

1882 TO UNDETERMINED TIME

Every person who, after public notice by the Superintendent General prohibiting the sale, gift or other disposal to Indians in any part of the province of Manitoba, Saskatchewan or Alberta, or the Territories, of any fixed ammunition or ball cartridge, without the permission in writing of the Superintendent General, sells or gives, or in any other manner conveys to any Indian, in the portion of the said provinces or Territories to which such notice applies, any fixed ammunition or ball cartridge, shall, on summary conviction before any stipendiary or police magistrate or by any two justices of the peace, or

by an Indian agent, be liable to a penalty not exceeding two hundred dollars, or to imprisonment for a
term not exceeding six months, or to both penalty and
imprisonment, within the limits aforesaid, at the discretion of the court before which the conviction is had.

Indian Act, 1880[2]

The root of the prohibition of ammunition was the fear
that if discontented Indians had ready access to repeat
rifles and fixed ammunition, the peaceful settlement of
the West and North would be hindered. The railway was
being pushed through and with it, along with settlers,
came traders who sold guns and ammunition to the Indians. There was a fear that if the Indians were armed, the
government would have serious difficulty in curtailing the
mounting agitation among western Indians and Métis.
The agitation they were concerned about eventually blew
up as the North-West Rebellion in 1885.

Around this time, and stemming from the same
motivation, the *Indian Act* was amended to allow the government to go beyond the Criminal Code and imprison
anyone found guilty of "having incited to riot three or
more Indians, non-treaty Indians or half-breeds."

The ammunition prohibition, the law against inciting
Indians, and the permit-to-pass system were all efforts
intended to divert further uprisings.

9 Prohibited the sale of intoxicants to Indians

1884 TO UNDETERMINED TIME

Every one who by himself, his clerk, servant or agent,
and every one who in the employment or on the

premises of another directly or indirectly on any pretense or by any device,

(a) sells, barters, supplies or gives to any Indian or non-treaty Indian, or to any person male or female who is reputed to belong to a particular band, or who follows the Indian mode of life, or any child of such person any intoxicant, or causes or procures the same to be done or attempts the same or connives thereat...

... shall, on summary conviction before any judge, police magistrate, stipendiary magistrate, or two justices of the peace or Indian agent, be liable to imprisonment for a term not exceeding six months and not less than one month, with or without hard labour, or to a penalty not exceeding three hundred dollars and not less than fifty dollars with costs of prosecution, or to both penalty and imprisonment in the discretion of the convicting judge, magistrate, justices of the peace or Indian agent.

Indian Act, 1884 amendment[3]

The early fur traders used alcohol, along with other items, to barter with Indians for furs. It was a common ploy to supply a great quantity of alcohol to the Indian traders prior to the negotiation process.

The earliest mentions of controlling Indians' access to alcohol that I have been able to determine was included in the instructions to superintendents, deputy superintendents, commissaries, interpreters, and missionaries in 1775.

Suppression of liquor sales to Indians became a fixture of the *Indian Act* legislation. In the Acts between 1884 and

1970, there are 39 references to intoxication, penalties for being intoxicated, for providing intoxicants, and for brewing intoxicants on reserves.

In 1884, it became a felony for Indians to purchase alcohol, consume alcohol, and enter a licensed establishment; likewise for anyone to sell alcohol to an Indian person. No form of prohibition has ever been 100 per cent effective. This particular prohibition created the scenario of Indians purchasing liquor from black market dealers and consuming it rapidly in back alleys and bushes.

In the early days of the *Indian Act*, one intent behind the alcohol ban was the belief that if Indians were able to access alcohol, they wouldn't be diligently working their "farmland." In other words, they should be on the reserve, working land that, in many cases, was not arable. They were expected to farm with rudimentary hand tools because they were denied access to modern farm tools, and if they did manage to grow anything, they weren't allowed to sell it without a permit to leave the reserve or the permit required to sell their produce.

The government and mainstream "society" also did not want to rub elbows with Indians in licensed drinking establishments, and the licensed establishments feared a decrease in customers.

During World War I and World War II, enlisted Indians were legally allowed to drink, but found upon their return to Canada that they were denied the same consideration at home. Indian veterans were banned from the Legions that their fellow, non-Indian soldiers frequented. Because of the prohibition, the Indian agent became the primary conduit of important information about benefits.

The Royal Commission on Aboriginal People noted the challenges for Indian veterans:

> Indian veterans had no access to veteran affairs admin-istrators, as we have seen, since personnel had taken over their responsibilities. In addition, Aboriginal vet-erans seldom had access to Royal Canadian Legion branches and newsletters. These were very helpful to most other veterans, informing them about the benefits available and helping them find out how to obtain them. In addition, they provided a useful means for discussing and comparing experiences on the subject. However, status Indians were usually barred from participation in the Legion, because Legions served alcohol, and Aboriginal men subject to the *Indian Act* could not attend functions where liquor was served. Exclusion of Indian veterans from Legions was extremely discrim-inatory, considering they had fought, been wounded and died alongside their non-Aboriginal comrades. But the *Indian Act* was inflexible on the issue of access to liquor. In only a few locations, such as Tyendinaga, did status Indians enjoy Legion membership. This exclu-sion served not only to separate Indian veterans from their wartime companions, but also jeopardized their receipt of veterans benefits.[4]

A Special Committee of the Senate and House of Commons studied the *Indian Act* between 1946 and 1948, and in that period they heard opinions from a broad spectrum of people regarding alcohol restrictions. In response to the findings of the Special Committee, the *Indian Act* underwent yet another set of amendments in

1951. The 1951 revision, rather than repeal the sections regarding prohibition of Indian intoxication, actually took it further by making it an offence for an Indian to be in possession of intoxicants or be intoxicated, whether on or off a reserve.

Saskatchewan, under Premier Tommy Douglas, followed the procedure and petitioned the federal government in 1960, with Douglas stating: "We are having this trouble because we are reaping the harvest of 50 years or more of making the Indian a second-class citizen. We are going to have to make up our minds whether we are going to keep the Indian bottled up in a sort of Canadian apartheid or whether we are going to let him become a good citizen." He cautioned, however, that while the Indian had been given equal rights, he had no more right to break the law than the white man. "If he is drunk or causing a disturbance, then he should be put out of the premises the same as a white man should. But he should not be put out just because he is an Indian."[5]

Indians would often consume their alcohol rapidly to avoid being arrested and fined. This led to the myth, which continues today, that Indians can't tolerate alcohol. The *Indian Act* prohibition set the stage for the pervasive stereotype that Indians suffered from an alcohol intolerance. It was a stereotype that played nicely into the federal government's stance that Indians were savages that needed to be "lifted up" or, more accurately, broken down, bit by bit.

Richard Thatcher, a sociologist who studied problem drinking in First Nations communities for over 20 years, has shown that most populations that are "dissembled by colonialism experience drug and alcohol problems." He has observed that it takes many generations to resolve these problems.[6]

What Thatcher says is supported by psychologist B.F. Skinner, who asserts that we are all products of our environment, and that we learn our values, behaviours, attitudes, and beliefs from the worlds in which we grow up. When we look at Indigenous populations through Skinner's lens, we can see that there has been a breakdown to the social fabric of communities as a result of Indian residential schools and Canadian Indian policies of assimilation. Indian children were taught in the schools that everything about them, their language, and their cultures was wrong. The parents and the children were affected by residential schools: the parents suffered the trauma of losing their children and the children suffered the trauma of feeling abandoned by their parents. This deeply rooted trauma caused many people to turn to alcohol as a coping mechanism, and it explains the alcoholism that we see present in Indigenous populations across the country.

Simply put, the *Indian Act* forcibly removed Indian children (usually from the ages of 6 to 16) from their families and communities to go to church-run, government-funded institutions geared specifically to assimilation. As a result, these children were not raised in kind, caring, loving families or communities. Instead they grew up in prison-like environments where they learned prisoner survivor skills, and most of the children were completely traumatized by the experience. Many survivors—and this is what they call themselves—came out and tried to cope with the breakdown in the core family and community environments. Some used alcohol and other means to cope, and have passed those behaviours down from generation to generation.

The breakdown in individual, family, and community values from generation to generation continues across the country, and that is why some Indigenous people and communities have problems with alcohol. For the record, it's something that many individuals and communities acknowledge, and they have begun to move down the path of what is often referred to as a "healing" process.

Discriminatory liquor offences on-reserve and off-reserve were repealed in 1985. With the passing of Bill C-31, band councils were given bylaw powers to control the sale and possession of liquor.

The systemic damage inflicted by the *Indian Act*'s prohibition laws of long ago continues to have an impact and define how mainstream society views Indians. Will that ever change?

10 Declared potlatch and other cultural ceremonies illegal
1884 TO 1951

This provision of the Indian Act was in place for close to 75 years and what that did was it prevented the passing down of our oral history. It prevented the passing down of our values. It meant an interruption of the respected forms of government that we used to have, and we did have forms of government be they oral and not in writing before any of the Europeans came to this country. We had a system that worked for us. We respected each other. We had ways of dealing with disputes.

JUDGE ALFRED SCOW, *1992*[7]

The federal government believed that true assimilation could be attained only by legally abolishing all cultural practices. Hence, under the *Indian Act*, the government created the potlatch law in 1884, making the potlatch and other cultural ceremonies, such as the Sun Dance, illegal.

Potlatch ceremonies were central to the culture of coastal Indians. They were held for a number of reasons, such as the passing of names, titles, and responsibilities of a chief to the eldest heir. Some cultures held potlatches to distribute wealth, establish rank, mark the passing of a chief or the head of a house, and celebrate weddings and births. Recognizing the potlatch as integral to the culture of coastal Indians, the government targeted it with particular force. Both the government and missionaries viewed potlatch ceremonies as excessive, wasteful, and barriers to assimilation. The concept of establishing rank by one's ability to share wealth rather than establish rank by holding on to wealth was alien to Europeans.

If the potlatch, the cornerstone of the culture of many coastal Indians, could be eradicated, the government believed the missionaries would be free to fill the cultural void with Christianity. Children in residential schools were taught that potlatches were outdated superstitions that led to poverty, and they were encouraged to not attend when home visiting. In reality all the potlatch ban did was drive the potlatch underground. The government severely underestimated Indians' resistance to losing the freedom to continue with traditions.

This excerpt from a letter from Duncan Campbell Scott to one of his western officials sums up how dismissive the government was of Indian culture: "It has always been clear to me that the Indians must have some sort of recreation, and if our agents would endeavour to substitute reasonable amusements for this senseless drumming and dancing, it would be a great assistance."[8]

One famous example of an underground potlatch took place at Christmas in 1921 in Alert Bay. 'Namgis Chief Dan Cranmer held a six-day potlatch to celebrate a wedding. The potlatch was held on Village Island in an effort to keep the activities hidden from the Indian agents and missionaries. Unfortunately, the celebration was detected, and under the potlatch law, 45 people were arrested and charged, and 22 people were jailed. Their crimes? Giving speeches, dancing, and gift giving. An additional injustice was that the community lost hundreds of priceless ceremonial items, including masks and regalia, which were confiscated and, over time, dispersed around the world to collectors and museums.

Potlatches continued to be held underground by a few determined communities, and the government eventually realized they were fighting a losing battle. Also, after World War II, the Canadian public became more aware of basic human rights and the appalling treatment of Indigenous Peoples. In 1951, the *Indian Act* was amended and the potlatch law was deleted. The first legal potlatch was hosted by Chief Mungo Martin in Victoria in 1952.

In the 71 years that the potlatch law was in effect, almost three generations grew up deprived of the cultural fabric of their ancestors, and thousands of irreplaceable ceremonial masks, robes, blankets, and other potlatch items were lost forever to their people.

11 Restricted Indians from leaving their reserve without permission from an Indian agent

1885 TO 1951 (NOT LEGISLATED BUT A POLICY CREATED IN 1885 AND ABANDONED IN 1951)

No rebel Indians should be allowed off the Reserves without a pass signed by an I.D. official. The dangers of complications with white men will thus be lessened and by preserving a knowledge of individual movements any inclination to petty depredations may be checked by the facility of apprehending those who commit such offences.

HAYTER REED, *Assistant Indian Commissioner, 1885*[9]

The Red River Rebellion (1869 to 1870) made it more challenging to encourage settlers to move to Saskatchewan, as they had concerns for their safety. The outbreak of the North-West Rebellion (1885) exacerbated those concerns. Prime Minister John A. Macdonald, keen to develop the agricultural potential of the West, needed a means of allaying the settlers' fears and inhibiting the ability of Indians to congregate. Despite the lack of a legal basis for restricting the movement of Indians, the prime minister readily endorsed the concept of a pass system when it was brought to his attention. Notices were posted on Treaty 6 reserves warning all Indians against leaving their reserves.

While it was never written into the *Indian Act* and the prime minister acknowledged that the legal ability to enforce it did not exist, the pass system was used effectively by Indian agents to control the movements of Indians. "In some cases, rations and other 'privileges' were withheld from those who refused to comply with pass regulations, but the most effective approach was to have the police arrest those found off the reserve without passes and, where possible, prosecute them either for trespass under the Indian Act or for vagrancy under the criminal code."[10]

A permit to pass included the time an individual was allowed to be off reserve, the purpose of the time away, and whether or not the individual was allowed to carry a gun. Indian agents knew well the attitudes and characters of all those who fell under their jurisdictions so could decline a request for a pass if they considered the applicant a potential threat. The pass system was initially used to control those who had participated in the Red River Rebellion but later expanded to apply to all Indians, although history suggests the permit-to-pass system was primarily administered in the Prairies.

In order to obtain a permit to pass, Indians would occasionally have to travel many days by foot to the Indian agent's house, not knowing if he would be there when they arrived. If the agent was away, they would either have to camp and wait, or return home. The pass system was also a means of maintaining a separation between Indians and the European farmers, which seems illogical considering the government's goal of assimilation—it's hard to achieve assimilation if the target population is isolated on reserves. The pass system restricted Indians' access to local towns in order to prevent Indian farmers from wasting their time when they should be tending their crops, which they were restricted from selling. The pass system additionally supported the government's attempts to quash potlatches, the Sun Dance, and other cultural practices.

Beginning in 1889, parents required passes to visit their children interned at residential schools. Controlling parents' access to their children aided and abetted the government's policy of keeping the family and their influence distanced from their children. Agents were encouraged to only provide a pass to parents to visit their children in school no more frequently than four times a year. If a child was ill, and the residential school shared this information with the child's parents, additional passes might be issued.

12 Created residential schools

1886 TO 1996 (FIRST DISCUSSED IN 1840S; LAST SCHOOL CLOSED IN 1996)

The Governor in Council may make regulations, which shall have the force of law, for the committal by justices or Indian agents of children of Indian blood under the age of sixteen years, to such industrial school or boarding school, there to be kept, cared for and educated for a period not extending beyond the time at which such children shall reach the age of eighteen years.

Indian Act, 1884[11]

And so it began: the most aggressive and destructive of all *Indian Act* policies. When the federal government signed the 11 numbered treaties starting in 1871, it assumed responsibility for the education of the Indians of Manitoba, Saskatchewan, and Alberta, as well as portions of Ontario, British Columbia, and the Northwest Territories. Indian signatories to the treaties realized that life as they knew it was seriously impacted by the influx of Europeans, and they wanted the children to have an education so they could take part in the new wage economy. They did not envision what lay ahead for their children at residential schools. How could they?

Residential schools brought immeasurable human suffering to the First Nations, Inuit, and Métis Peoples, the effects of which continue to reverberate through generations of families and many communities. Other policies were harsh but could be worked around. The government banned the potlatch, so practitioners went underground to continue to hold ceremonies; the government pushed people onto small reserves but they still were with their families. But when the government took the children from their families, it was unbearable.

The goal of the schools was to "kill the Indian in the child,"[12] but tragically it was the children themselves who died in overwhelming numbers at these schools. It is estimated that 6,000 of the 150,000 children who attended the schools between the 1870s and 1996 either died or disappeared. The numbers are not precise because no one kept accurate records: not the schools, the churches that managed the schools, or the Indian agents. Children died at the schools from disease, malnourishment, and broken hearts. Many children who escaped from their residential school died on the journey to their home community.

The government did not have a clear policy on discipline, which frequently was in the form of beating and whipping, in the schools, and discipline was arbitrary and harsh. Indian Affairs Deputy Minister Hayter Reed gave these directions to his staff:

> Instructions should be given, if not already sent, to the Principals of the various schools, that children are not to be whipped by anyone save the Principal, and even when such a course is necessary, great discretion should be used and they should not be struck on the head, or punished so severely that bodily harm might ensue. The practice of corporal punishment is considered unnecessary as a general measure of discipline and should only be resorted to for very grave offences and as a deterrent example.[13]

In 1914, Duncan Campbell Scott, Deputy Superintendent General of Indian Affairs, acknowledged that the system was open to criticism. He said, "Insufficient care was exercised in the admission of children to the schools. The well-known predisposition of Indians to tuberculosis resulted in a very large percentage of deaths among the pupils. They were housed in buildings not carefully designed for school purposes, and these buildings became infected and dangerous to the *inmates.*" What's remarkable is that he also acknowledged how many children died at residential schools: "*It is quite within the mark to say that fifty per cent of the children who passed through these schools did not live to benefit from the education which they had received therein*"[14] [emphasis added].

Prior to the 1876 *Indian Act*, education was provided at day schools built on reserves for the children to attend and begin their assimilation into settler society, but low attendance impeded this plan. Nicholas Flood Davin was commissioned to study how the Americans handled the education of native children and provided a report. In 1879 he produced the *Report on Industrial Schools for Indians and Halfbreeds*, which became known as the *Davin Report.* The report asserted that if assimilation was to be successful, then it had to start when the child was young, that the schools should be far removed from the home community in order to nullify the influence of the parents, and that their mythology should be replaced with Christianity.

The government revised its policy based on the *Davin Report* and abandoned on-reserve schools in favour of off-reserve, dormitory-style, industrial schools. The government preferred this new system because it separated the children from their parents, thereby allowing for the full indoctrination of the children into Christian beliefs and customs to kill the Indian in the child. Prime Minister John A. Macdonald said to the House of Commons in 1883:

> When the school is on the reserve the child lives with its parents, who are savages; he is surrounded by savages, and though he may learn to read and write, his habits, and training and mode of thought are Indian. He is simply a savage who can read and write. It has been strongly pressed on myself, as the head of the Department, that Indian children should be withdrawn as much as possible from the parental influence, and the only way to do that would be to put them in central training industrial schools where they will acquire the habits and modes of thought of white men.[15]

In 1920, the Act was amended to combat ongoing frustration over low attendance by making it compulsory for status Indian children to attend residential schools. If parents or guardians did not readily hand over their children to the Indian agent, the *Indian Act* gave power to the agent to enter the family home and seize the children, often with the help of the local constabulary or by the constabulary alone. Parents or guardians who tried to hide the children were liable to be arrested and or imprisoned. The 1927 *Indian Act* stated:

> Any parent, guardian or person with whom an Indian child is residing who fails to cause such child, being between the ages aforesaid, to attend school as required by this section after having received three days notice so to do by a truant officer shall, on the complaint of the truant officer, be liable on summary conviction before a justice of the peace or Indian agent to a fine of not more than two dollars and costs, or imprisonment for a period not exceeding ten days or both, and such child may be arrested without a warrant and conveyed to school by the truant officer: Provided that no parent or other person shall be liable to such penalties if such child, (a) is unable to attend school by reason of sickness or other unavoidable cause; (b) has passed the entrance examination for high schools; or, (c) has been excused in writing by the Indian agent or teacher for temporary absence to assist in husbandry or urgent and necessary household duties.[16]

The Act stated that children could be excused if they were diligently employed in the schools' farms or "necessary household duties," such as cooking and cleaning. The children often worked in the fields to raise products for sale to offset costs, or they cooked or cleaned more frequently than they had lessons in classroom. Their education often degenerated into exploited child labour.

Missing school for traditional pursuits was forbidden. In reality, every aspect of the children's former lives was forbidden: they were not allowed to speak their language, practise their traditions, or dress in their own clothing. They could visit their families only during Christian holidays, and only if the parents were compliant with certain rules.

Here is a copy of a letter sent to parents whose children were interned in the Kamloops Indian Residential School. It shows the many rules parents were expected to follow:

KAMLOOPS INDIAN RESIDENTIAL SCHOOL
KAMLOOPS, B.C.
November 18, 1948

Dear Parents,
It will be your privilege this year to have your children spend Christmas at home with you. The holidays will extend from DECEMBER 18th to JANUARY 3rd. This is a privilege which is being granted if you observe the following regulations of the Indian Department.

I. THE TRANSPORTATION TO THE HOME AND BACK TO THE SCHOOL MUST BE PAID BY THE PARENTS. The parents must come themselves to get their own children. If they are unable to come they must send a letter to the Principal of the school stating that the parents of other children from the same Reserve may bring them home. The children will not be allowed to go home alone on the train or bus.

2. THE PARENTS MUST BRING THE CHILDREN BACK TO SCHOOL

If the children are not returned to School on time they will not be allowed to go home for Christmas next year.

I ask you to observe the above regulations in order that this privilege of going home for Christmas may be continued from year to year. It will be a joy for you to have your children with you for Christmas. It will be a joy also for your children and it will bring added cheer and happiness to your home.

Yours sincerely,
Rev. F. O'Grady, O.M.I.,
Principal

The schools, primarily managed by Anglican, Roman Catholic, Presbyterian, and United churches and a government wanting to shed the financial responsibility of Indians, were chronically underfunded. The buildings were drafty and unsanitary and food for the children was insufficient and often rotten. To augment the finances of the schools, the Act included a statute that allowed the government to collect any treaty annuities due to the children and use the money to maintain the school that the child attended.

The schools were also breeding grounds for diseases such as tuberculosis and influenza. The children, suffering

from the trauma of the absolute loss of everything famil-
iar in their lives, had severely impacted immune systems,
which left them vulnerable to disease. It is well known
that fear, anxiety, and depression brought on by a dra-
matic change in environment and lifestyles can have an
adverse impact on the immune system.

The children who simply could not survive in this
harsh and terrifying environment died at such a rate that
it came to the attention of Dr. Peter Bryce, a medical
doctor who was hired by the Department of the Interior
to manage public health issues in both the Immigration
Department and Indian Affairs. In 1907, Bryce released
his *Report on the Indian Schools of Manitoba and the North-
West Territories*. The report provided grim facts regarding
the devastating effects of tuberculosis on the children and
recommendations on how to improve the standards of
the schools to stem the spread of the disease both in the
schools and in the home communities of the students.

Bryce's report was never published by the Department of Indian Affairs, quite likely due to its damning
nature and recommendations for expensive renovations.
Most of Bryce's recommendations were rejected by the
Department of Indian Affairs as too costly and not align-
ing with the government's policy for rapid, affordable
assimilation.

In 1907, the same year that Bryce made his report, the
national magazine *Saturday Night* reported on residential
schools, observing that "Indian boys and girls are dying
like flies... Even war seldom shows as large a percentage of fatalities as does the education system we have
imposed on our Indian wards."[17]

The Deputy Superintendent General of Indian Affairs at the time of Bryce's report was Duncan Campbell Scott. In 1910, a few years after Bryce's recommendations, Scott reasserted his support for residential schools in a letter to the British Columbia Indian Agent General:

> It is readily acknowledged that Indian children lose their natural resistance to illness by habituating so closely in the residential schools, and that they die at a much higher rate than in their villages. But this alone does not justify a change in the policy of this Department, which is geared towards a *final solution* of our Indian Problem.[18] [emphasis added]

Bryce, who was committed to protecting and educating Indigenous children, later wrote *The Story of a National Crime: Being an Appeal for Justice to the Indians of Canada; the Wards of the Nation, Our Allies in the Revolutionary War, Our Brothers-in-Arms in the Great War.* In this slim publication Bryce included some of the letters between himself and Duncan Campbell Scott and commented on Scott's folly in not acting on his and others' recommendations: "In this particular matter, he is counting upon the ignorance and indifference of the public to the fate of the Indians; but with the awakening of the health conscience of the people, we are now seeing on every hand, I feel certain that serious trouble will come out of the departmental inertia, and I am not personally disposed to have any blame fall upon me."[19]

Residential schools are not ancient history. The last one closed in 1996, and attendance was mandatory until 1969. The legacy of intergenerational impacts on

Indigenous Peoples will continue for many generations to come.

In 1998, with the "Statement of Reconciliation," the federal government acknowledged the damage inflicted upon First Nations, Inuit, and Métis Peoples and put Canada on the slow, painful path of reconciliation with its shameful relationship with Indigenous Peoples. It was not until 2008, however, that a formal apology, which opens with "The treatment of children in Indian Residential Schools is a *sad chapter* in our history..." [emphasis added] was delivered by then Prime Minister Stephen Harper. (See page 84 for the full transcript of the apology.)

Following the formal apology, the Truth and Reconciliation Commission of Canada (TRC) began its six-year journey across the country, gathering statements from tens of thousands of survivors who had attended the residential schools. In 2015, the TRC produced *Honouring the Truth, Reconciling for the Future Summary of the Final Report of the Truth and Reconciliation Commission of Canada* and the associated 94 Calls to Action on this sad chapter on residential school policies. (See Appendix 3 for the full list of the Calls to Action.)

In the report, the TRC uses the term "cultural genocide" to describe the federal government's policies. The term "cultural genocide" was also used by former Supreme Court Chief Justice Beverley McLachlin in a speech in 2015. She said, "The most glaring blemish on the Canadian historic record relates to our treatment of the First Nations that lived here at the time of colonization." After an initial period of interreliance and equality, she said, Canada developed an "ethos of exclusion and cultural annihilation. 'Indianness' was not to be tolerated; rather it must be eliminated. In the buzz-word of the day, assimilation; in the language of the 21st century, cultural genocide."[20]

The United (1986), Anglican (1993), and Presbyterian (1994) churches have also made formal apologies. In 2009, Pope Benedict XVI expressed his "sorrow" to an Assembly of First Nations delegation for the abuse and "deplorable" treatment that Indigenous students suffered at Roman Catholic Church–run residential schools.

So, what has become of the 139 buildings that functioned as schools? The majority of the buildings have been torn down, and it's my understanding that fewer than 10 remain standing. Some of the remaining buildings have been renovated and now act as cultural and learning centres. The school that my father and other family members and friends attended, St. Michael's Indian Residential School in Alert Bay, BC, was torn down on February 18, 2015.

But the apprehension of children from family and community did not end when the government began closing residential schools in the 1950s. The 1960s saw an expansion of the child welfare system, and "by the end of the 1960s, '30 to 40 per cent of the children who were legal wards of the state were Aboriginal children—in stark contrast to the rate of 1 per cent in 1959.'"[21] In what is known as the Sixties Scoop, babies and children were taken from their parents and placed in boarding schools or with Euro-Canadian families. "Children continue to be apprehended at alarming rates under circumstances deemed to be 'child neglect' that are instead related to issues of poverty."[22] The Sixties Scoop continued until the 1980s.

The legacy of the residential school system continues to impact Indigenous people, families, and communities. On its doorstep we can lay the responsibility for the high poverty rates, the large number of Indigenous children in foster care, the disproportionate number of incarcerated Indigenous people, and the hundreds of missing and murdered Indigenous women.

"They rose against us"[1]

We have done all we could to put them on themselves; we have done all we could to make them work as agriculturists; we have done all we could, by the supply of cattle, agricultural implements and instruction, to change them from a nomadic to an agricultural life. We have had very considerable success; we have had infinitely more success during our short period, than the United States have had during twenty-five years. We have had a wonderful success; but still we have had the Indians; and then in these half-breeds, enticed by white men, the savage instinct was awakened; the desire of plunder—aye, and, perhaps, the desire of scalping—the savage idea of a warlike glory, which pervades the breast of most men, civilised or uncivilised, was aroused in them, and forgetting all the kindness that had been bestowed upon them, forgetting all the gifts that had been given to them, forgetting all that the Government, the white people and the Parliament of Canada had been doing for them, in trying to rescue them from barbarity; forgetting that we had given them reserves, the means to cultivate those reserves, and the means of education how to cultivate them—forgetting all these things, they rose against us.

JOHN A. MACDONALD, *1885*[2]

13 Forbade Indian students from speaking their home language

LATE 1880S TO EARLY 1960S

It was through language that children received their cultural heritage from parents and community. It was the vital connection that civilizers knew had to be cut if progress was to be made.

Royal Commission on Aboriginal Peoples, 1996[3]

When most children entered the residential school system, they primarily spoke their home language. However, when they crossed the threshold of these imposing buildings, all they knew, including their language, was forbidden. The educators were given the mandate that the children had to learn to read, write, understand, and speak English at all costs. Punishment for speaking their language ranged from the relatively mild practice of washing their mouths out with soap to the inconceivable punishment of piercing of their tongues with sewing needles.

When children returned home for a visit or finished school, they frequently felt alien in their families because they had been taught that their language, culture, and traditions were evil. Many were so traumatized by the punishments received for speaking their home language, they could not bring themselves to speak it at home. The fear of speaking meant the children kept to themselves the horrors they experienced while away at school. Another outcome was that when residential school survivors became parents, they taught their children English so that they would not suffer the same punishments when they were taken off to residential schools.

It's difficult to determine when the shift away from punishment for speaking home language started. An educated guess would place it in the late 1940s. A shift away from punishing students for speaking their home language did not equate to the introduction of instruction in Indigenous languages in the schools. By 1967 just nine Saskatchewan residential schools reported "an emphasis on relating course content to the Indian culture as imaginative and a sign of progress in making the educational experience meaningful for the Indian child."[4] Many generations suffered from the trauma of not being allowed to speak their Indigenous language and, as a result, many Indigenous languages today are in severe danger of disappearing. In 1996, the United Nations Educational, Scientific and Cultural Organization (UNESCO) declared that Canada's Aboriginal languages were among the most endangered in the world.

According to Statistics Canada, in 2011 approximately one in six Aboriginal people were able to use an Aboriginal language in conversation. This translates to 240,815 Aboriginal people, or 17.2 per cent, of the population, a decline of 2 per cent since 2006.

In oral societies, when the words are gone, so are the histories, the value systems, the spiritual, ecological knowledge, the worldviews, the stories and the songs. It is an irreplaceable loss. The loss of a language severs the connection between a people and their culture.

14 Forbade western Indians from appearing in any public dance, show, exhibition, stampede, or pageant wearing traditional regalia
1906 TO 1951

Any Indian in the province of Manitoba, Saskatchewan, Alberta or British Columbia, or in the Territories who participates in any Indian dance outside the bounds of his own reserve, or who participates in any show, exhibition, performance, stampede or pageant in aboriginal costume without the consent of the Superintendent General or his authorized agent, and any person who induces or employs any Indian to take part in such dance, show, exhibition, performance, stampede or pageant, or induces any Indian to leave his reserve or employs any Indian for such a purpose, whether the dance, show, exhibition, stampede or pageant has taken place or not, shall on summary conviction be liable to a penalty not exceeding twenty-five dollars, or to imprisonment for one month, or to both penalty and imprisonment.

Indian Act, 1906[5]

The early 1900s was the era in which there was a growing trend of inviting Indians to dance at agricultural exhibitions as novelty acts. The prohibition of having Indians participate in a public event was in keeping with other punitive efforts of the federal government to prevent Indians, in every way possible, from expressing their culture and from congregating. As this was an indictable offence, it was outside the jurisdiction of Indian agents acting as justices of the peace. This oversight was rectified in 1918 by bringing the offences under the umbrella of the Indian agent. In 1933, the prohibition was rewritten to omit the wearing of regalia. Indians merely participating in the event without permission was enough to incur a penalty.

15 Leased uncultivated reserve lands to non-Indians
1918 TO 1985

We would be only too glad to have the Indian use this land, if he would... But he will not cultivate this land, and we want to cultivate it; that is all.

ARTHUR MEIGHEN, *Minister of the Interior and Superintendent of Indian Affairs, 1918*[6]

In the late 1800s settlers were flooding into the Prairies and their demand for land put pressure on the government to open up unused (uncultivated) land. In 1894, the *Indian Act* was amended to allow for reserve land held by physically disabled Indians, widows, orphans, or others who could not cultivate their lands to be leased out, and to do so without band approval or surrender of title. What the government ignored, or failed to understand, was that just because land was not cultivated did not mean it was not being used. Uncultivated land provided crucial habitat for the animals and plants that had sustained Indians for generations.

Leasing of land without approval or surrender opened the door to encouraging bands to consent to surrender their land. Under the *Indian Act*, reserve land could not be acquired by the Crown without consent of the bands concerned. Government negotiators told bands that the money from selling their land would alleviate poverty and clear up debt. Members of the band were told they were eligible for 10 per cent of the land sale. When there wasn't the anticipated uptake, the *Indian Act* was amended in 1906 to increase that 10 per cent to 50 per cent. Government negotiators were said to have attended meetings "with strongboxes of cash."[7]

In the period from 1896 to 1911, 21 per cent of reserve land in the Prairie provinces was surrendered to accommodate western expansion. Following World War I in 1918 there was an additional clamour for reserve land. The government wanted soldiers settled on the land, and some of the best land available was reserve land. Parliament introduced legislation that authorized the Soldier Settlement Board to acquire reserve land.

The new rush for land followed closely on the heels of the rush to arrange leases on reserve land for settlers. The government was then in the position of having to cancel those leases as the land couldn't be surrendered if there was an active lease on it. Leases were suddenly considered a hindrance rather than an aid to breaking up reserves. If Indians were getting an income from the leases, they were unlikely to be interested in relinquishing that income.

After World War I, it is regrettable that Department of Indian Affairs officials, and those in government, did not foresee problems of livelihood and occupation for Indian reserve residents in an era when land, agriculture, and stock-raising were the foundations of the Prairie economy. It is all the more disturbing that the federal government, assigned to protect and conserve the interests and estates of those defined as "Indian," eagerly offered up this land, helping to create the impression that it was "open season" on Indian reserve land and successfully diverting attention away from the vacant land held out of production by powerful corporations.

Following World War II there was another need for land for returning soldiers, but by this time the Department of Indian Affairs was having sober second thoughts. One official stated that consent to the surrender of Indian reserve land had been given "rather unwisely" in the past "when as a matter of fact, having in mind future development and requirements, such lands should have been retained for Indian use."[8]

Leasing of reserve land and surrenders of reserve land are immense topics that have resulted in significant legal challenges and awards for First Nation communities. This is but a brief synopsis of some of the main points.

16 Forbade Indians from forming political organizations
1927 TO 1951

Prior to World War I, Indians had few means of connecting with other communities so they had no idea if the conditions and treatment they were subjected to was standard practice or unique. Ironically, it was fighting in a war on a distant continent that brought them together.

Although Indians were exempt from conscription because they were not considered "citizens" of Canada and did not have the right to vote, an estimated 4,000 Indigenous people enlisted in World War I. They enlisted as a means of escaping the harsh living conditions on the reserve and to protect their treaty rights. An additional motivation was the fear that if the Allies lost the war, the treaties held with the Crown would cease to exist.

Being stationed together overseas was the first time Indigenous people from different communities across Canada had an opportunity to discuss their living conditions on reserves. They talked about the expropriation of reserve land, the restrictions and hardships they experienced due to government policies, and their treatment at the hands of the federal government representatives. One of those listening and sharing was Lieutenant Frederick Loft, a Mohawk from the Six Nations Band. While stationed abroad, Loft managed to arrange a meeting with the Privy Council and the King of England to describe the living conditions of Indian people in Canada.

When he returned to Canada, Loft wrote to chiefs inviting them to meetings and asking them to share the information with as many others as possible. He explained his vision of the League of Indians of Canada: that Indians needed to be unified to pursue common goals of recognized land rights, better living conditions, and better education. He advocated for annual fees to cover expenses and having the surplus go to a fund for Indian children to attend high school. He also expressed his intent to work with the federal government. The first three annual meetings were held in Ontario (1919), Manitoba (1920), and Saskatchewan (1921). As the largest interest base was in the West, further meetings were held in that region.

The concept of Indians communicating with one another and forming a unified group was met with distrust on the part of the federal government, and Indian agents were instructed to attend the meetings. Duncan Campbell Scott, Deputy Superintendent General of Indian Affairs, was wary that any sort of unification of First Nations would be contrary to their assimilation in mainstream society. Scott was sufficiently disturbed by Loft and the League of Indians of Canada that he attempted to have Loft involuntarily enfranchised (stripped of his classification as a status Indian).

J.D. MacLean, the Assistant Deputy and Secretary, wrote to an Indian agent, "I would state that you should warn your Indians that it is not in their interests to encourage any Indian of another reserve to come amongst them with the object of disaffecting them against the government. If you find that such anyone uses seditious language it might be advisable to lay an information against him before a magistrate."[9]

In retaliation, the government amended the *Indian Act* in 1927 to ban Indians from forming political organizations like the Leagues of Indians. Not surprisingly, an amended *Indian Act* did not put an end to Indian political organizations; some organizations continued to meet to discuss their rights but they did so underground. Thomas King, author of *The Inconvenient Indian*, writes:

> So it shouldn't come as any surprise that the League of
> Indians of Canada didn't last very long. And given the

generous attitudes and encouragements of the government, another Native political organization wouldn't be attempted until after World War II. Of course, Indian political organizations didn't disappear just because the government didn't like them. They went underground. One story I've heard is that at the beginning of some of these political meetings, to avoid the possibility of prosecution, the participants would sing "Onward Christian Soldiers." If anyone asked, they could say they belonged to a Bible study group. I don't know if this is a true story, but I believe it. More than that, I like it. It makes us sound downright... subversive.[10]

17 Prohibited anyone, Indian or non-Indian, from soliciting funds for Indians to hire legal counsel
1927 TO 1951

Every person who, without the consent of the Superintendent General expressed in writing, receives, obtains, solicits or requests from any Indian any payment or contribution or promise of any payment or contribution for the purpose of raising a fund or providing money for the prosecution of any claim which the tribe or band of Indians to which such Indian belongs, or of which he is a member, has or is represented to have for the recovery of any claim or money for the benefit of the said tribe or band, shall be guilty of an offence and liable upon summary conviction for each such offence to a penalty not exceeding two hundred dollars and not less than fifty dollars or to imprisonment for any term not exceeding two months.

Indian Act, 1927[11]

The emergence of Indian organizations in the 1920s to pursue land claims spurred the federal government to look for further means of tightening their stranglehold. The response was to amend the *Indian Act* with Section 141 and other amendments. This made it illegal for Indians to hire lawyers or raise money to hire legal counsel. It also meant jail sentences for anyone who lent Indians money for lawyers or legal counsel. This amendment, coupled with it being illegal for Indians to form political organizations, created a very real barrier to Indians pursuing land claims and human rights actions. The federal government was trying desperately to plug the holes on the dyke, knowing that if the dam burst and all the pent-up resentment and anger was given a voice, their control over Indians would be severely weakened.

In *Conspiracy of Legislation: The Suppression of Indian Rights in Canada* (1991), authors Chief Joe Mathias and Gary R. Yabsley observed: "Indian nations were therefore denied those fundamental rights that are taken for granted in any democratic system. They were, as a matter of colonial and provincial policy, denied rights to lands they had occupied for centuries. This exclusion from the land was extended through the discriminatory provisions of colonial and provincial land legislation. And they were prohibited by federal law [from] seeking a legal remedy for this injustice."[12]

18 Prohibited pool hall owners from allowing Indians entrance

1927 TO UNDETERMINED TIME

Where it is made to appear in open court that any Indian, summoned before such court, by inordinate frequenting of a pool room either on or off a reserve, misspends or wastes his time or means to the detriment of himself, his family or household, of which he is a member, the police magistrate, stipendiary magistrate, Indian agent, or two justices of the peace holding such court, shall by writing under his or their hand or hands forbid the owner or person in charge of a pool room which such Indian is in the habit of frequenting to allow such Indian to enter such pool room for the space of one year from the date of such notice.

Any owner or person in charge of a pool room who allows an Indian to enter a pool room in violation of such notice, and any Indian who enters a pool room where his admission has been so forbidden, shall be liable on summary conviction to a penalty not exceeding twenty-five dollars and costs or to imprisonment for a term not exceeding thirty days.

Indian Act, 1930[13]

The *Indian Act* also directed where Indians were allowed to seek amusement. By prohibiting Indians from going to pool rooms, the government was ensuring they did not amuse themselves in the same pursuits as non-Indians. Indians were expected to spend the majority of their time engaged in industrious pursuits as opposed to leisure pursuits. It was acceptable for non-Indians to go to licensed establishments, play pool, or go to dances, but it was not acceptable for Indians. The powers that be were concerned that Indians would be spending time in a pool room when they should be on the reserve or in school. Idle time in towns was not conducive to an Indian progressing towards self-sufficiency.

The *Indian Act, 1985* continues a form of control in that the Governor General has the authority to make regulations regarding the operation, supervision, and control of pool rooms, dance halls, and other places of amusement on-reserve.[14]

{ 5 }

And Its Days Are Numbered

It is the opinion of the writer that... the Government will in time reach the end of its responsibility as the Indians progress into civilization and finally disappear as a separate and distinct people, not by race extinction but by gradual assimilation with their fellow-citizens.

DUNCAN CAMPBELL SCOTT, *Deputy Superintendent General of Indian Affairs, 1931*[1]

19 Forbade Indian students from practising their traditional religion
1940S

In 1947, Roman Catholic official J. O. Plourde told a federal parliamentary committee that since Canada was a Christian nation that was committed to having "all its citizens belonging to one or other of the Christian churches," he could see no reason why the residential schools "should foster aboriginal beliefs." United Church official George Dorey told the same committee that he questioned whether there was such a thing as "native religion."

Truth and Reconciliation Commission of Canada, 2016[2]

Christian faith-based settlers and policy makers generally were dismissive of Indigenous spirituality and creation beliefs. They considered Indians heathens who needed to be shown the light of Christianity in order to raise themselves up from their lives of savagery.

The federal government used residential schools to denigrate cultural beliefs. As the schools were run in partnerships between the government and churches, religious instruction at the schools was very much the mainstay of the day. Children were taught to kneel and pray in the religious denomination of the school.

When these children returned home, they frequently felt disassociated from their family and culture after many years of being told that their former lives were invalid and their spirituality and beliefs were pagan and primitive. Many generations of residential school survivors have struggled with the very real sense that they do not belong to either their community or the world beyond their community.

Mary Courchene, a student at the residential schools at Fort Alexander in Manitoba and Lebret in Saskatchewan, describes the alienation she felt when she returned home: "And I looked at my dad, I looked at my mom, I looked at my dad again. You know what? I hated them. I just absolutely hated my own parents. Not because I thought they abandoned me; I hated their brown faces. I hated them because they were Indians."[3]

The dismissal of Indigenous spiritual beliefs contributed to the erosion of Indigenous cultures. The loss of culture and connection to the land experienced today by Indigenous people is considered a contributing factor to the high rate of suicide in Indigenous communities.

20 Denied Indians the right to vote
UNTIL 1960

The right to vote, which most Canadians take for granted, was a hard-fought battle for Indigenous Peoples. In most parts of Canada, Indians were offered the right to vote at the time of Confederation—but only if they gave up their treaty rights and Indian status. Understandably, few were willing to do this. Métis people were not excluded from voting as few were covered by treaties and there was nothing to justify disqualifying them. Inuit were excluded from voting and no steps were taken to grant them the right to vote as most communities were geographically isolated. In the absence of special efforts to enable them to vote, the Inuit had no means of exercising the right.

Long before contact with Europeans, and the ensuing *Indian Act*, Indigenous Peoples had elaborate systems of government, so understandably many viewed the 19th-century proposal for enfranchisement unfavourably for two reasons: First, it would mean the termination of their recognition as distinct Nations or peoples (as signified by treaties with France, Great Britain, and later, Canada). This would mean the beginning of their assimilation into the settler society. And second, it would mean voting in a system of government that was alien to the traditions, conventions, and practices of governance of many Indian communities. Voting was also considered redundant as a traditional, effective system was already in place for choosing leaders and governing Nations.

Proposals to offer the franchise date back to at least 1885, when the federal government passed the *Electoral Franchise Act*, which gave the right to vote to Indian men. This Act was repealed in 1898 because the popular view at the time was that as Indians did not own property or pay taxes, they were not responsible enough to have a say in the choosing of the government. Here are some other reasons offered up in debates in the House of Commons:

- Indians were incapable of exercising the franchise.

- Indians were not capable of civilization and would eventually become extinct.

- Indians were utterly incapable of managing their own affairs, and the numerous legal disabilities imposed on them by the *Indian Act* made extension of the franchise inappropriate.

- There should be no representation without taxation.

- The vote should not be extended to Indians involved in the 1885 rebellion.

- Indian property interests in reserve lands were not equivalent to non-native property interests.

- Indians should not have the vote while under the discretionary care of the government.

- Indians were too controlled by government and therefore interference by Indian agents was possible.

- The true intent of the bill was gerrymandering.

- Extending the vote to Indians represented an encroachment on the rights of white men.[4]

The status quo endured for nearly a century, as there was little pressure to extend the franchise, although it was extended in 1924 to Indian veterans of World War I.

The fact that so many Indigenous people served with distinction in World War II was one of the reasons that the federal government concluded that the time had come for all Indigenous Peoples to have the full rights of citizenship after the war ended. The horrors of World War II made Canadians aware of human rights and that there were people on their own soil—the very people who had contributed so much to the Allied victory—who were living in appalling conditions. A parliamentary committee, at the urging of the voting public, was struck and made the recommendation in 1948 that the right to vote be extended to all Indigenous Peoples. The federal government extended the franchise to Inuit, who did not have treaties or reserves so were legally considered "ordinary citizens," but it balked at giving an unconditional vote to Indians. It remained a requirement that Indians waive their rights as status Indians before being granted the right to vote. There was little pressure from status Indians for the right to vote given the significance of what they were asked to forfeit in exchange. Also, as discussed in #1, "Imposed the elected chief and council system," there was a general antipathy towards voting in federal elections as Indians had their own, culturally based systems for choosing leaders and self-governing structures.

It was not until 1960, under the leadership of Prime Minister John Diefenbaker, that the right to vote was extended, unconditionally, to all Indigenous Peoples.

21 Is a piece of legislation created under colonial rule for the purpose of subjugating a group of people

Subjugate 1. Bring (a country, people etc.) into subjection; conquer

2. Bring under domination or control; make subservient or dependent

Oxford Canadian Dictionary

When the Royal Proclamation was issued in 1763, it laid the groundwork for what should have been as positive a relationship as possible between settlers and Indigenous Peoples. Of particular importance are the passages which state:

It is just and reasonable and essential to our Interest, and the Security of our Colonies, that the several Nations or Tribes of Indians with whom We are connected, and who live under our Protection, should not be molested or disturbed in the Possession of such parts of our Dominions and Territories as not having been ceded to or purchased by Us, are reserved to them, or any of them, as their Hunting Grounds... any Lands whatever, which, not having been ceded to or purchased by Us as aforesaid, are reserved to the said Indians, or any of them...

And We do hereby strictly forbid, on Pain of our Displeasure, all our loving Subjects from making any

Purchases or Settlements whatever, or taking Possession of any of the Lands above reserved, without our especial leave and Licence for that Purpose first obtained.

And We do further strictly enjoin and require all Persons whatever who have either wilfully or inadvertently seated themselves upon any Lands within the Countries above described or upon any other Lands which, not having been ceded to or purchased by Us, are still reserved to the said Indians as aforesaid, forthwith to remove themselves from such Settlements.[5]

This section of the Royal Proclamation is important because it recognizes the First Nations or Tribes of Indians as owners of the lands that the Europeans were using and occupying, and it sets out what today are sometimes called "special" hunting rights. The idea of "nations" comes from King George III and his colonial government and confirms the international convention of the day that colonizing countries should conduct government business with the inhabitants on a nation-to-nation basis and recognize the inhabitants as owners of the lands.

As I wrote in my book *Working Effectively with Indigenous Peoples*®, these ideas began to unravel with the passage of the *British North America Act* (now known as the *Constitution Act*), which officially made Canada a country in 1867. Following Section 91(24) of the Act, the federal government was given authority to make laws about Indians and lands reserved for the Indians. The Act marked a significant change in Indian policy from a nation-to-nation relationship to one in which Indians were considered wards of the Crown who should be forced to assimilate into mainstream society. The Act introduced an era that has reigned for over 150 years, and was to have a lasting impact on the Canadian state.

The tragic reality is that what should have been a positive and respectful code of conduct degenerated over time into one in which government policies led to cultural genocide, assimilation, theft of land, denial of treaty and constitutional rights, racism, and increasingly punitive laws meant to control every aspect of the lives and deaths of the original inhabitants of what is now Canadian territory.

If Canada and Canadians are going to reconcile with Indigenous Peoples, then the existing relationship—the one based on the *Indian Act*—has to be rebuilt. The past cannot be overlooked or dismissed as "ancient history," because it isn't; the impacts of the past are ongoing. The formal apology from Prime Minister Stephen Harper to residential school survivors and their families in 2009 was a much-needed first step.

Here's the transcript:

11 June 2008
Ottawa, Ontario
Statement of Apology

The treatment of children in Indian Residential Schools is a sad chapter in our history.

For more than a century, Indian Residential Schools separated over 150,000 Aboriginal children from their families and communities. In the 1870s, the federal government, partly in order to meet its obligation to educate Aboriginal children, began to play a role in the development and administration of these schools. Two primary objectives of the Residential Schools system were to remove and isolate children from the influence of their homes, families, traditions and cultures, and to assimilate them into the dominant culture. These objectives were based on the assumption Aboriginal cultures and spiritual beliefs were inferior and unequal. Indeed, some sought, as it was infamously said, "to kill the Indian in the child." Today, we recognize that this policy of assimilation was wrong, has caused great harm, and has no place in our country.

One hundred and thirty-two federally-supported schools were located in every province and territory, except Newfoundland, New Brunswick and Prince Edward Island. Most schools were operated as "joint ventures" with Anglican, Catholic, Presbyterian or United Churches. The Government of Canada built an educational system in which very young children were often forcibly removed from their homes, often taken far from their communities. Many were inadequately fed, clothed and housed. All were deprived of the care and nurturing of their parents, grandparents and communities. First Nations, Inuit and Métis languages and cultural practices were prohibited in these schools. Tragically, some of these children died while attending residential schools and others never returned home.

The government now recognizes that the consequences of the Indian Residential Schools policy were profoundly negative and that this policy has had a lasting and damaging impact on Aboriginal culture, heritage and language. While some former students have spoken positively about their experiences at residential schools, these stories are far overshadowed by tragic accounts of the emotional, physical and sexual abuse and neglect of helpless children, and their separation from powerless families and communities.

The legacy of Indian Residential Schools has contributed to social problems that continue to exist in many communities today.

It has taken extraordinary courage for the thousands of survivors that have come forward to speak publicly about the abuse they suffered. It is a testament to their resilience as individuals and to the strength of their cultures. Regrettably, many former students are not with us today and died never having received a full apology from the Government of Canada.

The government recognizes that the absence of an apology has been an impediment to healing and reconciliation. Therefore, on behalf of the Government of Canada and all Canadians, I stand before you, in this Chamber so central to our life as a country, to apologize to Aboriginal peoples for Canada's role in the Indian Residential Schools system.

To the approximately 80,000 living former students, and all family members and communities, the Government of Canada now recognizes that it was wrong to forcibly remove children from their homes and we apologize for having done this. We now recognize that it was wrong to separate children from rich and vibrant cultures and traditions that it created a void in many lives and communities, and we apologize for having done this. We now recognize that, in separating children from their families, we undermined the ability of many to adequately parent their own children and sowed the seeds for generations to follow, and we apologize for having done this. We now recognize that, far too often, these institutions gave rise to abuse or neglect and were inadequately controlled, and we apologize for failing to protect you. Not only did you suffer these abuses as children, but as you became parents, you were powerless to protect your own children from suffering the same experience, and for this we are sorry.

The burden of this experience has been on your shoulders for far too long. The burden is properly ours as a Government, and as a country. There is no place in Canada for the attitudes that inspired the Indian Residential Schools system to ever prevail again. You have been working on recovering from this experience for a long time and in a very real sense, we are now joining you on this journey. The Government of Canada sincerely apologizes and asks the forgiveness of the Aboriginal peoples of this country for failing them so profoundly.

Nous le regrettons
We are sorry
Nimitataynan
Niminchinowesamin
Mamiattugut

In moving towards healing, reconciliation, and resolution of the sad legacy of Indian Residential Schools, implementation of the Indian Residential Schools Settlement Agreement began on September 19, 2007. Years of work by survivors, communities, and

Aboriginal organizations culminated in an agreement that gives us a new beginning and an opportunity to move forward together in partnership.

A cornerstone of the Settlement Agreement is the Indian Residential Schools Truth and Reconciliation Commission. This Commission presents a unique opportunity to educate all Canadians on the Indian Residential Schools system. It will be a positive step in forging a new relationship between Aboriginal peoples and other Canadians, a relationship based on the knowledge of our shared history, a respect for each other and a desire to move forward together with a renewed understanding that strong families, strong communities and vibrant cultures and traditions will contribute to a stronger Canada for all of us.

On behalf of the Government of Canada
The Right Honourable Stephen Harper,
Prime Minister of Canada

But it turns out it was just words, and the trouble with words is they can be empty, and Indigenous Peoples have heard a lot of empty words since Confederation. Just one year after reading the apology, Stephen Harper spoke at the G20 meeting in 2009 and said: "We also have no history of colonialism. So we have all of the things that many people admire about the great powers but none of the things that threaten or bother them."[6]

You can see why there may be a sense of cynicism on the part of some Indigenous Peoples when it comes to promises and apologies. There's a lot of work to be done to untangle the relationship, but I have faith that it is indeed possible.

The White Paper

> We do not want the Indian Act retained because it is
> a good piece of legislation. It isn't. It is discriminatory
> from start to finish. But it is a lever in our hands and
> an embarrassment to the government, as it should be.
> No just society and no society with even pretensions to
> being just can long tolerate such a piece of legislation,
> but we would rather continue to live in bondage under
> the inequitable Indian Act than surrender our sacred
> rights. Any time the government wants to honour its
> obligations to us we are more than ready to help devise
> new Indian legislation.
>
> HAROLD CARDINAL, *The Unjust Society, The Tragedy
> of Canada's Indians, 1969*[7]

Over its history of cultural genocide and attempted
assimilation, the *Indian Act* targeted the most vulnerable,
controlled identity and membership, and attempted to
destroy traditions and culture. The Act fundamentally
distorted the traditional role of leadership by dismissing
cultural traditions regarding leaders and inserting the federal government into community politics. However, some
First Nations are hesitant to support removal of the *Indian
Act* because the Act both represents the duties owed the
Crown and protects inherent rights.

There was an attempt to abolish the Act in 1969 when
the government, under the leadership of Prime Minister
Pierre Trudeau, released the "Statement of the Government of Canada on Indian Policy," otherwise known as
the White Paper. At issue were *Indian Act* policies that
the government perceived to be both exclusionary and
discriminatory.

The fundamental goals of the White Paper were to eliminate "Indian" as a distinct legal status, repeal the *Indian Act*, void all treaties between Indigenous Peoples and Canada, and dismantle the Department of Indian Affairs. It intended to make all Indigenous Peoples "equal" to other Canadians by removing their distinctiveness as a People and their relationship to the land, and forcing them to assimilate into mainstream society with no Aboriginal or treaty rights whatsoever.

The White Paper elicited an unanticipated wrath of opposition from Indigenous Peoples. They felt that its terms were unacceptable and they found its tone both paternalistic and accusatory. Here are a few excerpts from the White Paper that may provide insight as to why there was vehement opposition to it.

From the Historical Background section:

> Before that time there had evolved a policy of entering into agreements with the Indians, of *encouraging them to settle on reserves* held by the Crown *for their use and benefit*, and of dealing with Indian lands through a separate organization—a policy of treating Indian people as a race apart. [emphasis added]

From the Treaties and Land Claims section:

> Many of the Indian people feel that successive governments have not dealt with them as fairly as they should. They believe that lands have been taken from them in an improper manner, or without adequate compensation, that their funds have been improperly administered, that their treaty rights have been

breached. Their sense of grievance influences their relations with governments and the community and limits their participation in Canadian life.

. . .

Many Indians look upon their treaties as the source of their rights to land, to hunting and fishing privileges, and to other benefits. Some believe the treaties should be interpreted to encompass wider services and privileges, and many believe the treaties have not been honoured. Whether or not this is correct in some or many cases, the fact is the treaties affect only half the Indians of Canada. Most of the Indians of Quebec, British Columbia, and the Yukon are not parties to a treaty.

The terms and effects of the treaties between the Indian people and the Government are widely misunderstood. A plain reading of the words used in the treaties reveals the limited and minimal promises which were included in them. As a result of the treaties, some Indians were given an initial cash payment and were promised land reserved for their exclusive use, annuities, protection of hunting, fishing and trapping privileges subject (in most cases) to regulation, a school or teachers in most instances and, in one treaty only, a medicine chest.

The right to hunt and fish for food is extended unevenly across the country and not always in relation to need. Although game and fish will become less and less important for survival as the pattern of Indian life continues to change, there are those who, at this time, still live in the traditional manner that their forefathers lived in when they entered into treaty with the government. The Government is prepared to allow such persons transitional freer hunting of migratory birds under the Migratory Birds Convention Act and Regulations.

The Government and the Indian people must reach a common understanding of the future role of the treaties. Some provisions will be found to have been discharged; others will have continuing importance. Many of the provisions and practices of another century may be considered irrelevant the light of a rapidly changing society and still others may be ended by mutual agreement. Finally, once Indian lands are securely within Indian control, the anomaly of treaties between groups within society and the government of that society will require that these treaties be reviewed to—how they can be equitably ended.

Other grievances have been asserted in more general terms. It is possible that some of these can be verified by appropriate research and may be susceptible of specific remedies. Others relate to aboriginal claims to land. These are so general and undefined it is not realistic to think of them as specific claims capable of remedy except through a policy and program that will end injustice to Indians as members of the Canadian community. This is the policy that the Government is proposing for discussion.[8]

When forced to withdraw the White Paper in 1970, Prime Minister Pierre Trudeau is said to have stated, "We'll keep them in the ghetto as long as they want."

DISMANTLING THE INDIAN ACT

The *Indian Act* has not achieved its goal of "getting rid of the Indian problem." Indigenous culture is openly celebrated by Indigenous and non-Indigenous people; the Indigenous population is the fastest growing segment of Canada; languages are being revived and recorded; and there are increasing instances of local governments recognizing original names of towns, sites, and streets. Indigenous communities and individuals are proudly rebuilding their nations.

So, after 150 years of rule, it's time to scrap the Act! What would that look like? In this next section we take a look at self-government and what that means.

{ 6 }

If Not the Indian Act, Then What?

IIIIIIIIIIIIIIIIIIIIIIIIIIIIIIIIIIIIIIIIIIIIIIIIII

I am often asked whether it would be better to change the existing Indian Act or to eliminate it entirely. Will we still need the Indian Act once our right to self-government is recognized and our treaties are implemented? I believe we will need some federal legislation to make clear the obligations the federal government bears towards First Nations peoples. This is radically different from an Indian Act that continues to allow a minister and some bureaucrats to tell people who they are, what they can do, or how they must live. That arrangement is a colonial relic. We would all like to see it disappear. But we would like to see the government fulfil its responsibilities to us, not shirk them by repealing the Indian Act and pretending that is the end of their obligations to First Peoples.

OVIDE MERCREDI, *former National Chief of the Assembly of First Nations, 1993*[1]

MANY BELIEVE THE answer is a return to Indigenous self-government. For Indigenous Peoples, self-government is seen as the foundation on which Nations are built. Self-government agreements are critical to communities that want to contribute to the discussions and participate in the decisions that affect their lives. One of the key recommendations from the *Report of the Royal Commission on Aboriginal Peoples* was that Indigenous Peoples have self-government:

> Aboriginal Peoples must have room to exercise their autonomy and structure their own solutions. The pattern of debilitating and discriminatory paternalism that has characterized federal policy for the past 150 years must end. Aboriginal people cannot flourish if they are treated as wards, incapable of controlling their own destiny...
>
> At the heart of our recommendations is recognition that Aboriginal Peoples are peoples, that they form collectivities of unique character, and that they have a right of governmental autonomy. Aboriginal Peoples have preserved their identities under adverse conditions. They have safeguarded their traditions during many decades when non-Aboriginal officials attempted to regulate every aspect of their lives. They are entitled to control matters important to their nations without intrusive interference. This autonomy is not something bestowed by other governments. It is inherent in their identity as peoples. But to be fully effective, their authority must be recognized by other governments.[2]

Indigenous self-government is often referred to as an "inherent" right that pre-existed long before European settlement. For this reason, some Indigenous Peoples balk at the concept of Canadian governments granting them self-government, because they believe the Creator gave them the responsibilities of self-government and that that right has never been surrendered; it was simply taken by government legislation. In this light, self-government does not have to be recognized by federal or provincial governments because the right continues to exist.

In August 1995, the government of Canada formally recognized the inherent right of self-government for Canada's Indigenous Peoples by releasing the *Federal Policy Guide: Aboriginal Self-Government—The Government of Canada's Approach to Implementation of the Inherent Right and the Negotiation of Aboriginal Self-Government* (Policy Guide). It stated:

> The Government of Canada recognizes the inherent right of self-government as an existing Aboriginal right under section 35 of the Constitution Act, 1982. It recognizes, as well, that the inherent right may find expression in treaties, and in the context of the Crown's relationship with treaty First Nations. Recognition of the inherent right is based on the view that the Aboriginal Peoples of Canada have the right to govern themselves in relation to matters that are internal to their communities, integral to their unique cultures, identities, traditions, languages and institutions, and with respect to their special relationship to their land and their resource"[3]

The Policy Guide makes it clear that all Indigenous self-government arrangements are to be negotiated with the federal government under the Policy Guide and will remain within the Canadian Constitution and subject to Canadian sovereignty:

> The inherent right of self-government does not include a right of sovereignty in the international law sense, and will not result in sovereign independent Aboriginal nation states. On the contrary, implementation of self-government should enhance the participation of Aboriginal Peoples in the Canadian federation, and ensure that Aboriginal Peoples and their governments do not exist in isolation, separate and apart from the rest of Canadian society.[4]

COMMUNITY HEALING AND SELF-GOVERNMENT

Most Indigenous Peoples recognize that self-government cannot serve as a panacea or silver bullet for the deep-rooted social, health, and economic problems that plague most Indigenous communities in Canada. The Royal Commission on Aboriginal Peoples heard considerable testimony from Indigenous women, many of whom stressed the need for healing in their communities. As Lynn Brooks, the Executive Director of the Status of Women Council of the Northwest Territories said in her testimony, "Most women supported fully the move toward self-government and yet had many concerns and fears about the fulfillment of that right for Aboriginal Peoples. Why? Why do women feel such ambivalence towards the idea of self-government? The answer is clear to women... We have to change our priorities. We must have personal and community healing."[5]

COMMON ELEMENTS OF SELF-GOVERNMENT

Generally speaking, a return to self-government shapes social and economic well-being and can include provisions for:

- Structure and accountability of Indigenous governments
- Revenues from land-based resources
- Financial resources from transfer payments (i.e. taxes) to fund the following, to name a few:
  - Education
  - Health care and social services
  - Police services
  - Law-making powers
  - Cultural preservation
  - Environmental protection
  - Land and resource governance
  - Housing
  - Property rights
  - Child welfare

In July 2017, the Department of Justice released the federal government's 10 Principles on Indigenous Peoples. Principles 4, 8, and 9, included below, are relevant to the self-government discussion:

4. *The Government of Canada recognizes that Indigenous self-government is part of Canada's evolving system of cooperative federalism and distinct orders of government.*

   This Principle affirms the inherent right of self-government as an existing Aboriginal right within section 35. Recognition of the inherent jurisdiction and legal orders of Indigenous nations is therefore the starting point of discussions aimed at interactions between federal, provincial, territorial, and Indigenous jurisdictions and laws.

As informed by the UN Declaration, Indigenous peoples have a unique connection to and constitutionally protected interest in their lands, including decision-making, governance, jurisdiction, legal traditions, and fiscal relations associated with those lands.

Nation-to-nation, government-to-government, and Inuit-Crown relationships, including treaty relationships, therefore include:

a. developing mechanisms and designing processes which recognize that Indigenous peoples are foundational to Canada's constitutional framework;

b. involving Indigenous peoples in the effective decision-making and governance of our shared home;

c. putting in place effective mechanisms to support the transition away from colonial systems of administration and governance, including, where it currently applies, governance and administration under the *Indian Act*; and

d. ensuring, based on recognition of rights, the space for the operation of Indigenous jurisdictions and laws.

8. *The Government of Canada recognizes that reconciliation and self-government require a renewed fiscal relationship, developed in collaboration with Indigenous nations, that promotes a mutually supportive climate for economic partnership and resource development.*

The Government of Canada recognizes that the rights, interests, perspectives, and governance role of

Indigenous peoples are central to securing a new fiscal relationship. It also recognizes the importance of strong Indigenous governments in achieving political, social, economic, and cultural development and improved quality of life.

This Principle recognizes that a renewed economic and fiscal relationship must ensure that Indigenous nations have the fiscal capacity, as well as access to land and resources, in order to govern effectively and to provide programs and services to those for whom they are responsible.

The renewed fiscal relationship will also enable Indigenous peoples to have fair and ongoing access to their lands, territories, and resources to support their traditional economies and to share in the wealth generated from those lands and resources as part of the broader Canadian economy.

A fairer fiscal relationship with Indigenous nations can be achieved through a number of mechanisms such as new tax arrangements, new approaches to calculating fiscal transfers, and the negotiation of resource revenue sharing agreements.

9. *The Government of Canada recognizes that reconciliation is an ongoing process that occurs in the context of evolving Indigenous–Crown relationships.*

This Principle recognizes that reconciliation processes, including processes for negotiation and implementation of treaties, agreements and other constructive arrangements, will need to be innovative and flexible and build over time in the context of evolving Indigenous-

Crown relationships. These relationships are to be guided by the recognition and implementation of rights.

Treaties, agreements, and other constructive arrangements should be capable of evolution over time. Moreover, they should provide predictability for the future as to how provisions may be changed or implemented and in what circumstances. Canada is open to flexibility, innovation, and diversity in the nature, form, and content of agreements and arrangements.

The Government of Canada also recognizes that it has an active role and responsibility in ensuring the cultural survival of Indigenous peoples as well as in protecting Aboriginal and treaty rights.

The Government of Canada will continue to collaborate with Indigenous peoples on changes to federal laws, regulations, and policies to realize the unfulfilled constitutional promise of s.35 of the *Constitution Act, 1982.*[6]

While self-government is not a quick fix for the deeply rooted social, health and economic issues that plague Indigenous communities, it is a step towards empowering communities to rebuild and heal from the intergenerational effects of residential schools.

{ 7 }

Looking Forward to a Better Canada

||||||||||||||||||||||||||||||||||||||||||||||||||||||||||||||||||||||||||||||||||||

CANADA IS CHANGING, and I foresee a future in which the *Indian Act* will be a chapter in Canada's history. To put it simply, the *Indian Act* was designed for a specific purpose that no longer exists in a country committed to reconciliation. The focus should now be on dismantling the *Indian Act*, moving towards self-government in an orderly and timely fashion, and creating a self-governing future for Indigenous Peoples outside of the *Indian Act*.

In addition to self-government, other important objectives that Indigenous Peoples will pursue in the absence of the *Indian Act* are a return to self-determination and self-reliance.

Self-determination is the right to decide who your people are. Under the *Indian Act* there are many rules governing membership, and bands/First Nations are required to maintain a registry of community members based on those membership rules. Self-determination would allow for both status and non-status members to be part of a self-governing community, which would be driven by the communities' own membership code.

Self-reliance means getting out of the perpetually underfunded arrangements currently offered by Canada. Indigenous communities need the opportunity to run efficient and self-sustaining communities by collecting their own revenue resource such as royalties and taxes from development on their lands, as well as collecting property taxes if so desired. This will allow communities to participate in the economic mainstream.

In August 2017, the federal government under Prime Minister Justin Trudeau dissolved Indigenous and Northern Affairs Canada, which, in various forms, has administered the *Indian Act* since 1876. In doing so, the government took action on a recommendation made in 1996 by the Royal Commission on Aboriginal Peoples.

> Over twenty years ago, the Royal Commission on Aboriginal Peoples acknowledged that a new relationship with Indigenous Peoples would require new structures. It recommended that we dramatically improve the delivery of services while accelerating a move to self-government and self-determination of Indigenous Peoples. One mechanism to achieve this was the *dissolution of INAC* and the creation of two new ministries to facilitate this work.
>
> We agree with the Royal Commission that rights recognition must be an imperative, and that is why today we are announcing the dissolution of INAC.
>
> In its place, we will be establishing two new departments: a Department of Crown–Indigenous Relations and Northern Affairs, and a Department of Indigenous

Services. These changes are modelled on the recommendations of the Royal Commission and will be finalized in cooperation with Indigenous Peoples...

What we are doing today is also a next step toward ending the *Indian Act*, but the pace of transition will also require the leadership of Indigenous communities themselves.

Today's announcement is an important step in building a true nation-to-nation, Inuit–Crown, and government-to-government relationship with First Nations, Inuit, and Métis peoples in Canada.[1] [emphasis added]

In the long term, the costs of maintaining the mandates of the current *Indian Act* are greater than the cost involved to dismantle the Act and provide the means for Indigenous communities to return to their former existence of self-government, self-determination, and self-reliance. While enforced cultural assimilation policies may have been abandoned decades ago, the effects and challenges are still ongoing. Removing the legislation that is the cause of many challenges will be good for all Canadians. It will be a giant step forward for Canada and Indigenous Peoples and a step that will contribute directly to reconciliation.

In the short term, if Canadians can stay committed to reconciliation, personally review the 94 recommendations drawn up by the Truth and Reconciliation Commission of Canada, and pursue the ones relevant to them, perhaps we could see the strengthening of the nation-to-nation relationship and create a better, more prosperous Canada that lives up to its fundamental ideology of recognition of human rights not just abroad but at home as well.

Terminology

IIIIIIIIIIIIIIIIIIIIIIIIIIIIIIIIIIIIIIIIIIIIIIIIIIIIIIIIIII

Aboriginal people/persons: More than one Aboriginal person.

Aboriginal people: Entire body of Aboriginal persons in Canada.

Aboriginal Peoples: Defined in the *Constitution Act, 1982* to include all Indigenous people of Canada: status Indians, non-status Indians, Métis, and Inuit.

Aboriginal Rights (as determined by Section 35 of the *Constitution Act, 1982*):
- are the practices, traditions, or customs that are integral to the distinctive culture of an Aboriginal society and were practised prior to European contact, meaning they were rooted in the pre-contact society.
- must be practised for a substantial period of time to have formed an integral part of the particular Aboriginal society's culture.
- must be an activity that is a central, defining feature that is independently significant to the Aboriginal society.

- must be distinctive, meaning it must be distinguishing and characteristic of that culture.
- must be given priority over all other land uses, after conservation measures.
- must meet a continuity requirement, meaning that the Aboriginal society must demonstrate that the connection with the land in its customs and laws has continued to the present day.
- may be the exercise in a modern form of an activity that existed prior to European contact (such as using vehicles to get to remote areas when hunting).
- may be regulated by government, but only by legislation explicitly directed at a compelling and substantial objective such as the conservation and management of natural resources.
- do not include an activity that exists solely because of the influence of European contact.
- do not include aspects of Aboriginal society that are true of every society such as eating to survive.

Aboriginal title: In general, refers to the rights of Aboriginal Peoples to the occupation, use, and enjoyment of their land and its resources. The classic legal definition was provided by the Supreme Court of Canada in *Delgamuukw v. British Columbia*:

> [A]boriginal title encompasses the right to *exclusive* use and occupation of land; second, aboriginal title encompasses *the right to choose* to what uses land can be put, subject to the ultimate limit that those uses cannot destroy the ability of the land to sustain future generations of Aboriginal Peoples; and third, that lands

held pursuant to aboriginal title have an inescapable *economic component.*

Band: The *Indian Act* defines "band" as a body of Indians for whose use and benefit in common lands have been set apart. Each band has its own governing band council, usually consisting of a chief and several councillors. The members of the band usually share common values, traditions and practices rooted in their language and ancestral heritage. Today, many bands prefer to be known as First Nations. Capitalize "Band" when it is part of a specific band, such as Osoyoos Indian Band; otherwise, use lowercase.

Band council or First Nation council: The band's governing body. Community members choose the chief and councillors by election under Section 74 of the *Indian Act*, or through traditional custom. The band council's powers vary with each band.

Chief: There are two classifications of chief:
- **Band chief:** A person elected by band members to govern for a specified term. Under the specifications of the *Indian Act*, First Nations must have an election every two years.
- **Hereditary chief:** A leader who has power passed down from one generation to the next along blood lines or other cultural protocols, similar to European royalty.

Enfranchisement: The process involved in giving up one's status as an Indian, which was predominant during era of Indian assimilation practices. In 1985, this practice was terminated by Bill C-31.

First Nation: A term that came into common usage in the 1970s to replace the term "Indian band," which many people found offensive. The term "First Nation" has been adopted to replace the word "band" in the names of many communities, and can refer to a single band, many bands, an Indigenous governing body organized and established by an Indigenous community, or an Indigenous community as a whole. First Nation is not applied to Inuit or Métis, who are distinct and separate.

First Peoples: Another, less frequently used collective term to describe the original peoples in Canada.

Indian: The legal identity of an Indigenous person who is registered under the *Indian Act*. The origin of the term "Indian" dates back to Christopher Columbus, who mistakenly thought he had reached the East Indies, so referred to the people in the lands he visited as *indios*, which is Spanish for "Indian." The term is now considered derogatory and outdated when used in reference to an individual, but it is still used in a historical and legal context. The term is still used:

- in direct quotations.
- when citing titles of books, works of art, etc.
- in discussions of history where necessary for clarity and accuracy.
- in discussions of some legal or constitutional matters requiring precision in terminology.
- in discussions of rights and benefits provided on the basis of "Indian" status.
- in statistical information collected using these categories (e.g., the Census).

Indian Act: The federal legislation that regulates Indians and reserves and sets out certain federal government powers and responsibilities towards First Nations and their reserved lands. The first *Indian Act* was passed in 1876, although there were a number of pre-Confederation and post-Confederation enactments with respect to Indians and reserves prior to 1876. Since then, the Act has undergone numerous amendments, revisions, and re-enactments. Indigenous and Northern Affairs Canada administers the *Indian Act.*

Indigenous Peoples: There is no generally accepted definition of Indigenous Peoples in a global context. Some countries refer to Indigenous Peoples as the people who were there first at contact. Others refer to Indigenous Peoples as the nomadic peoples within their borders. In Canada and in this book, we use a definition of Indigenous Peoples as Indian, Inuit, and Métis Peoples. This mirrors the constitutional terminology of Aboriginal Peoples as stated in Section 35.

Inherent rights: Pre-existing rights that a person is born with into their nation; officially recognized by Canada under Section 35 of the *Constitution Act, 1982.* Aboriginal Peoples of Canada strive for the inherent right to govern themselves in relation to matters that are internal to their communities; on matters integral to their unique cultures, identities, traditions, languages and institutions; and with respect to their special relationship to their land and their resources.

Inuit: Indigenous people in northern Canada, living mainly in Nunavut, Northwest Territories, northern Quebec, and Labrador. Ontario has a very small Inuit population. Inuit are not covered by the *Indian Act*. The federal government has entered into several major land claim settlements with Inuit. Usage: The word "Inuit" means "the people" in the Inuit language and is used when Inuit are referring to themselves as a culture. "Inuit" is also the plural form of "Inuk." Avoid using the term "Inuit people" or "the Inuit people" as that is redundant; "Inuit" is the preferred form.

Land claims: In 1973, the federal government recognized two broad classes of claims—comprehensive and specific.

- **Comprehensive claims:** Claims based on the assessment that there may be continuing Aboriginal rights to lands and natural resources. These kinds of claims come up in those parts of Canada where Aboriginal title has not previously been dealt with by treaty and other legal means. While each claim is unique, frequently these claims include such things as land title; fishing, trapping, and resource rights; and financial compensation.
- **Specific claims:** Claims that declare grievances over Canada's alleged failures to discharge specific obligations to First Nations groups.

Land claim agreement: A term used by the federal government to refer to a negotiated settlement with a First Nation on lands, land usage, and other rights.

Membership: Classification criteria (traditional or not) created by a community that defines who is a member of that community.

Métis: People of mixed Aboriginal and European ancestry. The Métis National Council adopted the following definition of "Métis" in 2002: "'Métis' means a person who self-identifies as Métis, is distinct from other Aboriginal peoples, is of historic Métis Nation Ancestry and who is accepted by the Métis Nation."

Non-status Indian: A legal term referring to any individual who for whatever reason is not registered with the federal government, or is not registered to a band which signed a treaty with the Crown.

Nation: People united by common descent, history, culture, and language associated with a particular territory.

Native: An outdated collective term referring to Indians (status and non-status), Métis, and Inuit. It has largely been replaced by "Aboriginal" or "Indigenous."

Reserve: Defined by the *Indian Act* as a "tract of land, the legal title to which is vested in Her Majesty, that has been set apart by Her Majesty for the use and benefit of a band." A result of the definition of reserve land in the *Indian Act* is that reserve land cannot be privately owned by the band or band members. "Reservation" is an American term.

Status Indian: An individual recognized by the federal government as registered under the *Indian Act*. A status Indian can be referred to as a "registered Indian," but "status Indian" is the more common term.

Surrender: A formal agreement that confirms the conditions and terms when a First Nation exchanges part of its territory for equitable compensation.

Traditional territory: The geographic area identified by a First Nation to be the area of land which they or their ancestors traditionally occupied or used.

Treaty: An agreement between government and a First Nation that defines the rights of Aboriginal Peoples with respect to lands and resources over a specified area, and may also define the self-government authority of a First Nation. Modern treaties, once ratified, become part of the law of the land.

Treaty Indian: Members of a community whose ancestors signed a treaty with the Crown and as a result are entitled to treaty benefits.

Treaty rights: Rights specified in a treaty. Rights to hunt and fish in traditional territory and to use and occupy reserves are typical treaty rights. This concept can have different meanings depending upon the context and perspective of the user. Treaty rights are constitutionally recognized and affirmed; the terms of treaties take precedence over the other laws and policies in Canada.

Treaty settlement land: The area of land that is part of a treaty and is therefore owned and managed by the First Nation that negotiated the treaty.

Tribal council: Usually refers to a group of bands working together to facilitate the administration and delivery of local services to their members. It is not defined under the *Indian Act.*

Indian Residential Schools: A Chronology

||||||||||||||||||||||||||||||||||||||||||||||||||||||||||||||||

A VERSION OF this chronology originally appeared in *LawNow* magazine in 2014. It was prepared by John Edmond, an Ottawa lawyer, who has updated it for this publication. John is a member of the Ontario and British Columbia bars who practised constitutional and Aboriginal law.

The chronology was compiled to convey, by historic milestones, how the Indian residential school system came to be, how it embodied attitudes of its time, how critics were dismissed, and how, finally, the deep harm it did to many members of generations of Indian children was exposed in the course of a reconciliation process that continues. While Canada is doing its best to compensate, in many senses, for the failings of the system, much of the damage to individuals, and to First Nations culture, can never be put right.

1755 Indian Department created as branch of British military to establish and maintain relations with Indians.

1820 This decade sees Anglican and Methodist missionary schools established in Upper Canada and Red River Settlement.

1842 Governor General Sir Charles Bagot appoints Commission to report on "the Affairs of the Indians in Canada."

1844 Bagot Commission finds reserve communities in a "half-civilized state"; recommends assimilationist policy, including establishment of boarding schools distant from child's community, to provide training in manual labour and agriculture; portends major shift away from Royal Proclamation of 1763 policy that Indians were autonomous entities under Crown protection.

1847 Dr. Adolphus Egerton Ryerson, Methodist minister and educational reformer, commissioned by the Assistant Superintendent General of Indian Affairs to study native education, supports Bagot approach (as does Governor General Lord Elgin); proposes model on which Indian Residential School system was built.

1856 "Any hope of raising the Indians ... to the ... level of their white neighbours, is yet a ... distant spark": Governor General Sir Edmund Head's Commission "to Investigate Indian Affairs in Canada."

1857 *Gradual Civilization Act* passed; males "sufficiently advanced in the elementary branches of education" can be enfranchised (they would no longer be "Indians," and could vote).

1861 St. Mary's Mission Indian Residential School, Mission, and Presbyterian Coqualeetza Indian Residential School, Chilliwack, the first residential schools in BC, established.

1862 Blue Quills Indian Residential School (Hospice of St. Joseph/Lac la Biche Boarding School) established at St. Paul, AB; first residential school on the Prairies.

1867 Confederation: *British North America Act* (now *Constitution Act, 1867*) establishes federal jurisdiction over Indians. Thus, while education is under provincial jurisdiction, Indian matters, including education, are federal.

Fort Providence and Fort Resolution Indian Residential Schools established; first residential schools north of 60.

1871 Treaty No. 1 entered into at Lower Fort Garry: "Her Majesty agrees to maintain a school on each reserve ... whenever the Indians of the reserve should desire it." This promise, repeated in subsequent treaties (though hedged in Treaties No. 5 on), reflected desire of Indian leadership to ensure transition of their youth to demands of anticipated newcomer society.

1876 *Indian Act* passed into law by Parliament.

1879 Nicholas Flood Davin, journalist and defeated Tory candidate, commissioned by Prime Minister Macdonald, also Minister of the Interior, to produce proposal for Indian education; visits U.S. industrial schools grounded in policy of "aggressive civilization"; produces *Report on Industrial Schools for Indians and Half-Breeds*. Four residential schools already operate in Ontario; "mission schools" are planned for the West. This date is generally taken to mark beginning of Indian Residential Schools, though the system had early predecessors in New France and New Brunswick, and several schools were already operating.

Duncan Campbell Scott, best known later as a "Confederation poet," joins Indian Affairs at age 17 as "copying clerk," at direction of Macdonald.

1883 First industrial school established at Battleford, modelled on the *Davin Report*.

1885 Residential schools said to be necessary to remove children from influence of the home as the only way "of advancing the Indian in civilization" (Lawrence Vankoughnet, Deputy Superintendent General, to Prime Minister Macdonald). Despite treaty promises, reserves lacked schools; removal, often forcible, of pupils to residential schools is the option chosen by government.

1890 Physician Dr. G. Orton reports to Indian Affairs that tuberculosis in the schools could be reduced by half; measures rejected as "too costly."

1892 Regulations passed giving control over daily school administration to churches: Catholic, Anglican, Presbyterian, Methodist. (In 1925, Methodists join most Presbyterians and others to form the United Church, which continues to run schools.)

1896 Programme of Studies issued; stresses importance of replacing "native tongue" with English. Children forbidden to speak their native language, even to each other, and punished for doing so. This continues to be the policy for the life of the system.

1904 Dr. Peter Bryce appointed "Medical Inspector" to the Departments of the Interior and Indian Affairs.

Minister Sir Clifford Sifton announces closure of industrial schools, large urban institutions, in favour of boarding schools. They are closed over the next two decades.

1907 Dr. Bryce visits 35 schools; reports appallingly unsanitary conditions, microorganism-bearing ventilation, high death rates; "the almost invariable cause" is tuberculosis.

"The appalling number of deaths among the younger children... brings the Department within unpleasant nearness to the charge of manslaughter" (Hon. S.H. Blake, K.C., Chair of Advisory Board on Indian Education, partner in what is now national law firm Blake, Cassels & Graydon, to Minister Frank Oliver).

1908 Indian Affairs Accountant F.H. Paget reports school buildings in bad condition.

1909 Duncan Campbell Scott appointed Superintendent of Indian Education.

1910 "I can safely say that barely half of the children in our Indian schools survive to take advantage of the education we are offering them" (Scott to Major D.M. McKay, Indian Affairs Agent General in BC).

The children "catch the disease... in a building... burdened with Tuberculosis Bacilli" (Duck Lake Indian Agent MacArthur).

1912 "... [I]n the early days of school administration... [t]he well-known predisposition of Indians to tuberculosis resulted in a very large percentage of deaths among the pupils… [F]ifty percent of the children who passed through these schools did not live to benefit from the education which they had received therein" (Scott, in an essay in the authoritative 22-volume *Canada and Its Provinces*).

1913 Scott appointed Deputy Superintendent General of Indian Affairs (deputy minister), reporting to Minister of the Interior and Superintendent General Dr. William A. Roche.

1919 Position of Medical Inspector for Indian Agencies and Residential Schools abolished (in the year of the Spanish flu) by Order-in-Council on recommendation of Scott "for reasons of economy."

1920 "I want to get rid of the Indian problem" (D.C. Scott to Parliamentary Committee). A Scott-instigated amendment to the *Indian Act*, with church concurrence, compelled school attendance of all children aged 7 to 15. Though no particular kind of school is stipulated, Scott favours residential schooling to eliminate the influences of home and reserve, and hasten assimilation.

1922 Dr. Bryce publishes *The Story of a National Crime: Being an Appeal for Justice to the Indians of Canada, the Wards of the Nation, Our Allies in the Revolutionary War, Our Brothers-in-Arms in the Great War*. He charges that, for 1894–1908, within five years of entry 30 per cent to 60 per cent of students had died, an avoidable mortality rate had healthy children not been exposed to children with tuberculosis: a "trail of disease and death has gone on almost unchecked by any serious efforts on the part of the Department of Indian Affairs." His 1907 recommendations on tuberculosis control were not given effect, he says, "owing to the active opposition of Mr. D.C. Scott."

1923 "Residential Schools" adopted as official term, replacing "boarding" (55) and "industrial" (16), housing 5,347 children.

1932 Scott retires as Deputy Superintendent General after more than 52 years in the department. The anthologist John Garvin writes that Scott's "policy of assimilating the Indians had been so much in keeping with the thinking of the time that he was widely praised for his capable administration." He embodied a fundamental contradiction: while a rigid and often heartless bureaucrat, "his sensibilities as a poet [were] saddened by the waning of an ancient culture" (*Canadian Encyclopedia*).

1939 9,027 children are in 79 residential schools run by Catholic (60%), Anglican (25%), United, and Presbyterian churches. "1939 [was] the approximate mid-point of the history of the system" (John S. Milloy, *A National Crime*).

1944 Consensus develops among senior Indian Affairs officials that integration into provincial systems should replace segregated Aboriginal education.

1951 *Indian Act* of 1876, with many amendments, repealed; replaced with modernized *Indian Act* (today's Act, with amendments) conceptually similar to previous Act.

1955 Jean Lesage, Minister of Northern Affairs and National Resources, department responsible for Inuit (then known as Eskimos), gets Cabinet approval for broad education policy in the North. General policy is to substitute settlements for nomadic life. A school is built at Chesterfield Inlet, followed by Coppermine, and 10 "hostels." Some Inuit had formerly been sent south to Indian Affairs schools. "Destitute" Métis were sometimes also enrolled.

1969 Indian Affairs takes over sole management of residential schools from churches. Indian Affairs Minister Jean Chrétien produces assimilationist "White Paper" to abolish Indian status; strongly opposed by Indian organizations. Alberta Indian Association produces *Citizens Plus*, known as "Red Paper," in response. "White Paper" retracted two years later.

1971 Blue Quills School, St. Paul, AB, becomes first Indian-run school, following month-long contentious occupation by elders and others.

1972 National Indian Brotherhood (NIB, predecessor of Assembly of First Nations) produces *Indian Control of Indian Education*, advocating greater band control of education on reserves; adopted the next year by government.

1975 Six residential schools close this year; 15 remain.

1976 NIB proposes amendments to *Indian Act* to provide legal basis for Indian control of education; rejected by government.

1978 National Film Board produces first film ever on residential schools: *Wandering Spirit Survival School*, about a non-traditional school organized by parents who had themselves survived residential schools.

1984 187 bands are operating own (day) schools, half in BC, the rest mainly on the Prairies.

1993 Archbishop Michael Peers, Primate of Anglican Church of Canada, apologizes to survivors of Indian residential schools on behalf of the Church.

1996 Gordon Indian Residential School, Punnichy, Saskatchewan, closes; last of 139 Indian Residential Schools in Canada.

Royal Commission on Aboriginal Peoples recommends public investigation into violence and abuses at residential schools. Report brings these issues to national attention.

1998 Minister of Indian Affairs Jane Stewart responds to the *Report of the Royal Commission on Aboriginal Peoples* with a wide-ranging "Statement of Reconciliation." Acknowledges government's "role" in residential schools; states, "sexual and physical abuse... should never have happened. To those of you who suffered this tragedy at residential schools, we are deeply sorry." Announces $350 million for "community-based healing." But express apology had to wait until 2008.

2001 Federal office of Indian Residential Schools Resolution Canada created to manage and resolve the large number of abuse claims filed by former students, resulting in 17 court judgments.

2003 National Resolution Framework launched, including Alternative Dispute Resolution process, an out-of-court process providing compensation and psychological support for former students who were physically or sexually abused or had been wrongfully confined.

2004 Assembly of First Nations (AFN) *Report on Canada's Dispute Resolution Plan to Compensate for Abuses in Indian Residential Schools* leads to resolution discussions.

RCMP Commissioner Giuliano Zaccardelli expresses sorrow for the Force's role in the residential school system.

2005 $1.9 billion compensation package announced to benefit former residential school students.

2007 Indian Residential Schools Settlement Agreement—largest class action settlement in Canadian history, negotiated and approved by parties and courts in nine jurisdictions—implemented. Of the 139 schools ultimately included in the settlement, 64 are Roman Catholic, 35 Anglican, 14 United Church, and the balance other or no denomination. The objective is reconciliation with the estimated 80,000 former students then still living, of over 150,000 enrolled since 1879.

Elements are:
- Common Experience Payment to be paid to all eligible former students who resided at a recognized Indian Residential School;
- Independent Assessment Process for claims of sexual or serious physical abuse;
- Establishment of a Truth and Reconciliation Commission;
- Commemoration Activities;
- Measures to support healing such as the Indian Residential Schools Resolution Health Support Program and an endowment to the Aboriginal Healing Foundation.

Survivors report harsh and cruel punishments; suicides of others; physical, psychological and sexual abuse; poor quality and meagre rations and shabby clothing in the schools; and inability on leaving to belong in either the Aboriginal or the larger world. Post-traumatic stress disorder, major depression, anxiety disorder, and borderline personality disorder have been diagnosed, and many have criminal records.

2008 Prime Minister Harper offers formal apology in Parliament for the Indian residential schools, in presence of Aboriginal delegates and church leaders. Indian Residential Schools Truth and Reconciliation Commission established June 1, with five-year mandate, later extended to 2015.

2009 AFN Chief Phil Fontaine meets Pope Benedict XVI at Vatican. Pope Benedict expresses "sorrow" and "sympathy and prayerful solidarity," but avoids apologizing.

After a rocky start, with resignations of original Commissioners, Truth and Reconciliation Commission begins work under Justice Murray Sinclair, an Aboriginal Manitoba judge who became the province's Associate Chief Justice in 1988.

2010 Truth and Reconciliation Commission begins hearings in Winnipeg.

2011 University of Manitoba President David Barnard apologizes to Truth and Reconciliation Commission of Canada for institution's role in educating people who operated the residential school system.

2012 Truth and Reconciliation Commission releases *Interim Report*: http://nctr.ca/assets/reports/TRC/Interim%20report%20English%20electronic.pdf

Reviews progress; explains statement gathering and document collection process. Tells of degrading treatment, unwarranted punishments, and physical and sexual abuse by "loveless institutions." Makes numerous recommendations respecting public education about residential schools and about mental health and wellness programs, especially in the North, and that Canada and churches establish a cultural revival fund. Notes mandate to establish a National Research Centre.

Over 105,000 applications for Common Experience Payments are received by Canada by 2012 deadline; over 79,000 are found eligible and paid, the average amount being $19,412.

September 19 is the final deadline for Independent Assessment Process claims.

2014 Commission's hearings in more than 300 communities wrap up. "National Events," in Winnipeg, Inuvik, Halifax, Saskatoon, Montreal, and Vancouver have been held, as required by the Settlement Agreement, the final one taking place March 27–30 in Edmonton.

2015 May 31–June 3: "Closing Event" held in Ottawa.

August 16: Plaque unveiled at Ottawa's Beechwood Cemetery, the National Cemetery of Canada, in honour of Dr. Peter Bryce (1853–1932), author of *The Story of a National Crime*.

November 1: Plaque at Beechwood Cemetery honouring Duncan Campbell Scott as a Confederation Poet modified to include mention of role in residential schools.

December 15: Truth and Reconciliation Commission releases massive and sweeping six-volume, 3,231-page *Final Report*. The TRC also produced a summary and five other companion volumes, 2012–15.

- The Report looks to the future: "Reconciliation is not about 'closing a sad chapter of Canada's past,' but about opening new healing pathways of reconciliation that are forged in truth and justice."

- Assimilation policy was cultural genocide, "the destruction of those structures and practices that allow [a targeted] group to continue as a group."

- At the heart of the Report are 94 "Calls to Action," under two main headings, "Legacy" and "Reconciliation." Governments, educational, professional and sports bodies, media, churches (including the Pope), the arts, and the corporate sector are called to action. "Legacy" Calls are to "redress the legacy of residential schools" in the areas of Child Welfare, Education, Language and Culture, Health, and Justice. Under "Justice," an "Investigation into missing and murdered Aboriginal women and girls" is called for, and this is underway. "Reconciliation" Calls are more general, the most numerous of which call for "full" adoption and implementation of the *United Nations Declaration on the Rights of Indigenous Peoples* "as the framework for reconciliation," and various related matters. This is controversial, and the federal government is equivocal. Other Calls are for a "Covenant of Reconciliation," a National Council for Reconciliation, Church apologies, and a National Day for Truth and Reconciliation as a statutory holiday. Many non-governmental entities, including the Law Societies of Upper Canada and British Columbia, have already acted in response to the Report.

2016 The Supreme Court of Newfoundland and Labrador approves a $50 million settlement of five class action lawsuits on behalf of Indigenous former students from Labrador who attended one of the residential schools at Cartwright (Lockwood), North West River (Yale), Makkovik and Nain (in Labrador), and St. Anthony (on the island of Newfoundland). The schools were established by the International Grenfell Association and the Moravian Mission well before 1949 when Newfoundland joined Canada, but subsequently received government support until the last one closed in 1980.

2017 Prime Minister Trudeau apologizes, at Happy Valley–Goose Bay, NL, to the Indigenous former students who attended residential schools in Newfoundland and Labrador, and to their "families, loved ones and communities impacted by these schools for the painful and sometimes tragic legacy these schools left behind." Residential school students in the province, having been excluded from the 2007 Indian Residential Schools Settlement Agreement, were excluded from Prime Minister Harper's 2008 apology.

This brief entry cannot do justice to this weighty set of documents; the reader is encouraged to refer to the *Summary of the Final Report*: http://nctr.ca/assets/reports/Final%20Reports/Executive_Summary_English_Web.pdf

On release of the *Final Report*, the Truth and Reconciliation Commission closes. Its legacy is taken up by National Centre for Truth and Reconciliation, located on the University of Manitoba's Fort Garry Campus in Winnipeg: http://umanitoba.ca/nctr.

Truth and Reconciliation Commission of Canada: Calls to Action

||||||||||||||||||||||||||||||||||||||||||||||||||||||||||||||||||

THE TRUTH AND Reconciliation Commission released its summary report and findings on June 2, 2015, after six years of hearings and testimony from more than 6,000 residential school survivors and their loved ones. The report includes 94 Calls to Action to be followed if Canada is to address the "cultural genocide" of Indigenous Peoples as enacted with the residential school policy and achieve true reconciliation. As is often stated, reconciliation is not an Indigenous problem, it's a Canadian problem, and every Canadian needs to be aware of this very dark (but not distant, as the last school closed in 1996) period of history, understand that it has caused a intergenerational and ongoing impact, and find ways and means to support reconciliation.

In the words of my father, Chief Robert Joseph, "We start today. We start with every little step. If we start right now, and this moment is a moment of reconciliation for some of us, it's a huge, huge achievement."

Here are the 94 Calls to Action in their entirety:

Calls to Action

In order to redress the legacy of residential schools and advance the process of Canadian reconciliation, the Truth and Reconciliation Commission makes the following calls to action.

Legacy

CHILD WELFARE

1 We call upon the federal, provincial, territorial, and Aboriginal governments to commit to reducing the number of Aboriginal children in care by:

i Monitoring and assessing neglect investigations.

ii Providing adequate resources to enable Aboriginal communities and child-welfare organizations to keep Aboriginal families together where it is safe to do so, and to keep children in culturally appropriate environments, regardless of where they reside.

iii Ensuring that social workers and others who conduct child-welfare investigations are properly educated and trained about the history and impacts of residential schools.

iv Ensuring that social workers and others who conduct child-welfare investigations are properly educated and trained about the potential for Aboriginal communities and families to provide more appropriate solutions to family healing.

v   Requiring that all child-welfare decision makers consider the impact of the residential school experience on children and their caregivers.

2   We call upon the federal government, in collaboration with the provinces and territories, to prepare and publish annual reports on the number of Aboriginal children (First Nations, Inuit, and Métis) who are in care, compared with non-Aboriginal children, as well as the reasons for apprehension, the total spending on preventive and care services by child-welfare agencies, and the effectiveness of various interventions.

3   We call upon all levels of government to fully implement Jordan's Principle.

4   We call upon the federal government to enact Aboriginal child-welfare legislation that establishes national standards for Aboriginal child apprehension and custody cases and includes principles that:

i   Affirm the right of Aboriginal governments to establish and maintain their own child-welfare agencies.

ii Require all child-welfare agencies and courts to take the residential school legacy into account in their decision making.

iii Establish, as an important priority, a requirement that placements of Aboriginal children into temporary and permanent care be culturally appropriate.

5   We call upon the federal, provincial, territorial, and Aboriginal governments to develop culturally appropriate parenting programs for Aboriginal families.

EDUCATION

6 We call upon the Government of Canada to repeal Section 43 of the *Criminal Code of Canada*.

7 We call upon the federal government to develop with Aboriginal groups a joint strategy to eliminate educational and employment gaps between Aboriginal and non-Aboriginal Canadians.

8 We call upon the federal government to eliminate the discrepancy in federal education funding for First Nations children being educated on reserves and those First Nations children being educated off reserves.

9 We call upon the federal government to prepare and publish annual reports comparing funding for the education of First Nations children on and off reserves, as well as educational and income attainments of Aboriginal peoples in Canada compared with non-Aboriginal people.

10 We call on the federal government to draft new Aboriginal education legislation with the full participation and informed consent of Aboriginal peoples. The new legislation would include a commitment to sufficient funding and would incorporate the following principles:

i   Providing sufficient funding to close identified educational achievement gaps within one generation.

ii Improving education attainment levels and success rates.

iii Developing culturally appropriate curricula.

iv Protecting the right to Aboriginal languages, including the teaching of Aboriginal languages as credit courses.

v   Enabling parental and community responsibility, control, and accountability, similar to what parents enjoy in public school systems.

vi Enabling parents to fully participate in the education of their children.

vii Respecting and honouring Treaty relationships.

11 We call upon the federal government to provide adequate funding to end the backlog of First Nations students seeking a post-secondary education.

12 We call upon the federal, provincial, territorial, and Aboriginal governments to develop culturally appropriate early childhood education programs for Aboriginal families.

LANGUAGE AND CULTURE

13 We call upon the federal government to acknowledge that Aboriginal rights include Aboriginal language rights.

14 We call upon the federal government to enact an Aboriginal Languages Act that incorporates the following principles:

i   Aboriginal languages are a fundamental and valued element of Canadian culture and society, and there is an urgency to preserve them.

ii Aboriginal language rights are reinforced by the Treaties.

iii The federal government has a responsibility to provide sufficient funds for Aboriginal-language revitalization and preservation.

iv The preservation, revitalization, and strengthening of Aboriginal languages and cultures are best managed by Aboriginal people and communities.

v Funding for Aboriginal language initiatives must reflect the diversity of Aboriginal languages.

15 We call upon the federal government to appoint, in consultation with Aboriginal groups, an Aboriginal Languages Commissioner. The commissioner should help promote Aboriginal languages and report on the adequacy of federal funding of Aboriginal-languages initiatives.

16 We call upon post-secondary institutions to create university and college degree and diploma programs in Aboriginal languages.

17 We call upon all levels of government to enable residential school Survivors and their families to reclaim names changed by the residential school system by waiving administrative costs for a period of five years for the name-change process and the revision of official identity documents, such as birth certificates, passports, driver's licenses, health cards, status cards, and social insurance numbers.

HEALTH

18 We call upon the federal, provincial, territorial, and Aboriginal governments to acknowledge that the current state of Aboriginal health in Canada is a direct result of previous Canadian government policies, including residential schools, and to recognize and implement the health-care rights of Aboriginal people as identified in international law, constitutional law, and under the Treaties.

19 We call upon the federal government, in consultation with Aboriginal peoples, to establish measurable goals to identify and close the gaps in health outcomes between Aboriginal and non-Aboriginal communities, and to publish annual progress reports and assess long-term trends. Such efforts would focus on indicators such as: infant mortality, maternal health, suicide, mental health, addictions, life expectancy, birth rates, infant and child health issues, chronic diseases, illness and injury incidence, and the availability of appropriate health services.

20 In order to address the jurisdictional disputes concerning Aboriginal people who do not reside on reserves, we call upon the federal government to recognize, respect, and address the distinct health needs of the Métis, Inuit, and off-reserve Aboriginal peoples.

21 We call upon the federal government to provide sustainable funding for existing and new Aboriginal healing centres to address the physical, mental, emotional, and spiritual harms caused by residential schools, and to ensure that the funding of healing centres in Nunavut and the Northwest Territories is a priority.

22 We call upon those who can effect change within the Canadian health-care system to recognize the value of Aboriginal healing practices and use them in the treatment of Aboriginal patients in collaboration with Aboriginal healers and Elders where requested by Aboriginal patients.

23 We call upon all levels of government to:

i   Increase the number of Aboriginal professionals working in the health-care field.

ii Ensure the retention of Aboriginal health-care providers in Aboriginal communities.

iii Provide cultural competency training for all health-care professionals.

24 We call upon medical and nursing schools in Canada to require all students to take a course dealing with Aboriginal health issues, including the history and legacy of residential schools, the *United Nations Declaration on the Rights of Indigenous Peoples*, Treaties and Aboriginal rights, and Indigenous teachings and practices. This will require skills-based training in intercultural competency, conflict resolution, human rights, and anti-racism.

JUSTICE

25 We call upon the federal government to establish a written policy that reaffirms the independence of the Royal Canadian Mounted Police to investigate crimes in which the government has its own interest as a potential or real party in civil litigation.

26 We call upon the federal, provincial, and territorial governments to review and amend their respective statutes of limitations to ensure that they conform to the principle that governments and other entities cannot rely on limitation defences to defend legal actions of historical abuse brought by Aboriginal people.

27 We call upon the Federation of Law Societies of Canada to ensure that lawyers receive appropriate cultural competency training, which includes the history and legacy of residential schools, the *United Nations Declaration on the Rights of Indigenous Peoples*, Treaties and Aboriginal rights, Indigenous law, and Aboriginal–Crown relations. This will require skills-based training in intercultural competency, conflict resolution, human rights, and anti-racism.

28 We call upon law schools in Canada to require all law students to take a course in Aboriginal people and the law, which includes the history and legacy of residential schools, the *United Nations Declaration on the Rights of Indigenous Peoples*, Treaties and Aboriginal rights, Indigenous law, and Aboriginal–Crown relations. This will require skills-based training in intercultural competency, conflict resolution, human rights, and antiracism.

29 We call upon the parties and, in particular, the federal government, to work collaboratively with plaintiffs not included in the Indian Residential Schools Settlement Agreement to have disputed legal issues determined expeditiously on an agreed set of facts.

30 We call upon federal, provincial, and territorial governments to commit to eliminating the overrepresentation of Aboriginal people in custody over the next decade, and to issue detailed annual reports that monitor and evaluate progress in doing so.

31 We call upon the federal, provincial, and territorial governments to provide sufficient and stable funding to implement and evaluate community sanctions that will provide realistic alternatives to imprisonment for Aboriginal offenders and respond to the underlying causes of offending.

32 We call upon the federal government to amend the Criminal Code to allow trial judges, upon giving reasons, to depart from mandatory minimum sentences and restrictions on the use of conditional sentences.

33 We call upon the federal, provincial, and territorial governments to recognize as a high priority the need to address and prevent Fetal Alcohol Spectrum Disorder (FASD), and to develop, in collaboration with Aboriginal people, FASD [prevention] programs that can be delivered in a culturally appropriate manner.

34 We call upon the governments of Canada, the provinces, and territories to undertake reforms to the criminal justice system to better address the needs of offenders with Fetal Alcohol Spectrum Disorder (FASD), including:

i Providing increased community resources and powers for courts to ensure that FASD is properly diagnosed, and that appropriate community supports are in place for those with FASD.

ii Enacting statutory exemptions from mandatory minimum sentences of imprisonment for offenders affected by FASD.

iii Providing community, correctional, and parole resources to maximize the ability of people with FASD to live in the community.

iv Adopting appropriate evaluation mechanisms to measure the effectiveness of such programs and ensure community safety.

35 We call upon the federal government to eliminate barriers to the creation of additional Aboriginal healing lodges within the federal correctional system.

36 We call upon the federal, provincial, and territorial governments to work with Aboriginal communities to provide culturally relevant services to inmates on issues such as substance abuse, family and domestic violence, and overcoming the experience of having been sexually abused.

37 We call upon the federal government to provide more supports for Aboriginal programming in halfway houses and parole services.

38 We call upon the federal, provincial, territorial, and Aboriginal governments to commit to eliminating the overrepresentation of Aboriginal youth in custody over the next decade.

39 We call upon the federal government to develop a national plan to collect and publish data on the criminal victimization of Aboriginal people, including data related to homicide and family violence victimization.

40 We call on all levels of government, in collaboration with Aboriginal people, to create adequately funded and accessible Aboriginal-specific victim programs and services with appropriate evaluation mechanisms.

41 We call upon the federal government, in consultation with Aboriginal organizations, to appoint a public inquiry into the causes of, and remedies for, the disproportionate victimization of Aboriginal women and girls. The inquiry's mandate would include:

i   Investigation into missing and murdered Aboriginal women and girls.

ii Links to the intergenerational legacy of residential schools.

42 We call upon the federal, provincial, and territorial governments to commit to the recognition and implementation of Aboriginal justice systems in a manner consistent with the Treaty and Aboriginal rights of Aboriginal peoples, the *Constitution Act, 1982*, and the *United Nations Declaration on the Rights of Indigenous Peoples*, endorsed by Canada in November 2012.

Reconciliation
CANADIAN GOVERNMENTS AND THE UNITED NATIONS
DECLARATION ON THE RIGHTS OF INDIGENOUS PEOPLE

43 We call upon federal, provincial, territorial, and municipal governments to fully adopt and implement the *United Nations Declaration on the Rights of Indigenous Peoples* as the framework for reconciliation.

44 We call upon the Government of Canada to develop a national action plan, strategies, and other concrete measures to achieve the goals of the *United Nations Declaration on the Rights of Indigenous Peoples*.

ROYAL PROCLAMATION AND COVENANT OF RECONCILIATION

45 We call upon the Government of Canada, on behalf of all Canadians, to jointly develop with Aboriginal peoples a Royal Proclamation of Reconciliation to be issued by the Crown. The proclamation would build on the Royal Proclamation of 1763 and the Treaty of Niagara of 1764, and reaffirm the nation-to-nation relationship between Aboriginal peoples and the Crown. The proclamation would include, but not be limited to, the following commitments:

i   Repudiate concepts used to justify European sovereignty over Indigenous lands and peoples such as the Doctrine of Discovery and *terra nullius*.

ii   Adopt and implement the *United Nations Declaration on the Rights of Indigenous Peoples* as the framework for reconciliation.

iii   Renew or establish Treaty relationships based on principles of mutual recognition, mutual respect, and shared responsibility for maintaining those relationships into the future.

iv   Reconcile Aboriginal and Crown constitutional and legal orders to ensure that Aboriginal peoples are full partners in Confederation, including the recognition and integration of Indigenous laws and legal traditions in negotiation and implementation processes involving Treaties, land claims, and other constructive agreements.

46 We call upon the parties to the Indian Residential Schools Settlement Agreement to develop and sign a Covenant of Reconciliation that would identify principles for working collaboratively to advance reconciliation in Canadian society, and that would include, but not be limited to:

i   Reaffirmation of the parties' commitment to reconciliation.

ii Repudiation of concepts used to justify European sovereignty over Indigenous lands and peoples, such as the Doctrine of Discovery and *terra nullius*, and the reformation of laws, governance structures, and policies within their respective institutions that continue to rely on such concepts.

iii Full adoption and implementation of the *United Nations Declaration on the Rights of Indigenous Peoples* as the framework for reconciliation.

iv Support for the renewal or establishment of Treaty relationships based on principles of mutual recognition, mutual respect, and shared responsibility for maintaining those relationships into the future.

v   Enabling those excluded from the Settlement Agreement to sign onto the Covenant of Reconciliation.

vi Enabling additional parties to sign onto the Covenant of Reconciliation.

47 We call upon federal, provincial, territorial, and municipal governments to repudiate concepts used to justify European sovereignty over Indigenous peoples and lands, such as the Doctrine of Discovery and *terra nullius*, and to reform those laws, government policies, and litigation strategies that continue to rely on such concepts.

SETTLEMENT AGREEMENT PARTIES AND THE UNITED NATIONS DECLARATION ON THE RIGHTS OF INDIGENOUS PEOPLES

48 We call upon the church parties to the Settlement Agreement, and all other faith groups and inter-faith social justice groups in Canada who have not already done so, to formally adopt and comply with the principles, norms, and standards of the *United Nations Declaration on the Rights of Indigenous Peoples* as a framework for reconciliation. This would include, but not be limited to, the following commitments:

i   Ensuring that their institutions, policies, programs, and practices comply with the *United Nations Declaration on the Rights of Indigenous Peoples*.

ii   Respecting Indigenous peoples' right to self-determination in spiritual matters, including the right to practise, develop, and teach their own spiritual and religious traditions, customs, and ceremonies, consistent with Article 12:1 of the *United Nations Declaration on the Rights of Indigenous Peoples*.

iii   Engaging in ongoing public dialogue and actions to support the *United Nations Declaration on the Rights of Indigenous Peoples*.

iv   Issuing a statement no later than March 31, 2016, from all religious denominations and faith groups, as to how they will implement the *United Nations Declaration on the Rights of Indigenous Peoples*.

49 We call upon all religious denominations and faith groups who have not already done so to repudiate concepts used to justify European sovereignty over Indigenous lands and peoples, such as the Doctrine of Discovery and *terra nullius*.

EQUITY FOR ABORIGINAL PEOPLE IN THE LEGAL SYSTEM

50 In keeping with the *United Nations Declaration on the Rights of Indigenous Peoples*, we call upon the federal government, in collaboration with Aboriginal organizations, to fund the establishment of Indigenous law institutes for the development, use, and understanding of Indigenous laws and access to justice in accordance with the unique cultures of Aboriginal peoples in Canada.

51 We call upon the Government of Canada, as an obligation of its fiduciary responsibility, to develop a policy of transparency by publishing legal opinions it develops and upon which it acts or intends to act, in regard to the scope and extent of Aboriginal and Treaty rights.

52 We call upon the Government of Canada, provincial and territorial governments, and the courts to adopt the following legal principles:

i   Aboriginal title claims are accepted once the Aboriginal claimant has established occupation over a particular territory at a particular point in time.

ii Once Aboriginal title has been established, the burden of proving any limitation on any rights arising from the existence of that title shifts to the party asserting such a limitation.

NATIONAL COUNCIL FOR RECONCILIATION

53 We call upon the Parliament of Canada, in consultation and collaboration with Aboriginal peoples, to enact legislation to establish a National Council for Reconciliation. The legislation would establish the council as an independent, national, oversight body with membership jointly appointed by the Government of Canada and national Aboriginal organizations, and consisting of Aboriginal and non-Aboriginal members. Its mandate would include, but not be limited to, the following:

i   Monitor, evaluate, and report annually to Parliament and the people of Canada on the Government of Canada's post-apology progress on reconciliation to ensure that government accountability for reconciling the relationship between Aboriginal peoples and the Crown is maintained in the coming years.

ii   Monitor, evaluate, and report to Parliament and the people of Canada on reconciliation progress across all levels and sectors of Canadian society, including the implementation of the Truth and Reconciliation Commission of Canada's Calls to Action.

iii Develop and implement a multi-year National Action Plan for Reconciliation, which includes research and policy development, public education programs, and resources.

iv   Promote public dialogue, public/private partnerships, and public initiatives for reconciliation.

54 We call upon the Government of Canada to provide multi-year funding for the National Council for Reconciliation to ensure that it has the financial, human, and technical resources required to conduct its work, including the endowment of a National Reconciliation Trust to advance the cause of reconciliation.

55 We call upon all levels of government to provide annual reports or any current data requested by the National Council for Reconciliation so that it can report on the progress towards reconciliation. The reports or data would include, but not be limited to:

i The number of Aboriginal children—including Métis and Inuit children—in care, compared with non-Aboriginal children, the reasons for apprehension, and the total spending on preventive and care services by child-welfare agencies.

ii Comparative funding for the education of First Nations children on and off reserves.

iii The educational and income attainments of Aboriginal peoples in Canada compared with non-Aboriginal people.

iv Progress on closing the gaps between Aboriginal and non-Aboriginal communities in a number of health indicators such as: infant mortality, maternal health, suicide, mental health, addictions, life expectancy, birth rates, infant and child health issues, chronic diseases, illness and injury incidence, and the availability of appropriate health services.

v Progress on eliminating the overrepresentation of Aboriginal children in youth custody over the next decade.

vi Progress on reducing the rate of criminal victimization of Aboriginal people, including data related to homicide and family violence victimization and other crimes.

vii Progress on reducing the overrepresentation of Aboriginal people in the justice and correctional systems.

56 We call upon the prime minister of Canada to formally respond to the report of the National Council for Reconciliation by issuing an annual "State of Aboriginal Peoples" report, which would outline the government's plans for advancing the cause of reconciliation.

PROFESSIONAL DEVELOPMENT AND TRAINING FOR PUBLIC SERVANTS

57 We call upon federal, provincial, territorial, and municipal governments to provide education to public servants on the history of Aboriginal peoples, including the history and legacy of residential schools, the *United Nations Declaration on the Rights of Indigenous Peoples*, Treaties and Aboriginal rights, Indigenous law, and Aboriginal–Crown relations. This will require skills-based training in intercultural competency, conflict resolution, human rights, and anti-racism.

CHURCH APOLOGIES AND RECONCILIATION

58 We call upon the Pope to issue an apology to Survivors, their families, and communities for the Roman Catholic Church's role in the spiritual, cultural, emotional, physical, and sexual abuse of First Nations,

Inuit, and Métis children in Catholic-run residential schools. We call for that apology to be similar to the 2010 apology issued to Irish victims of abuse and to occur within one year of the issuing of this Report and to be delivered by the Pope in Canada.

59 We call upon church parties to the Settlement Agreement to develop ongoing education strategies to ensure that their respective congregations learn about their church's role in colonization, the history and legacy of residential schools, and why apologies to former residential school students, their families, and communities were necessary.

60 We call upon leaders of the church parties to the Settlement Agreement and all other faiths, in collaboration with Indigenous spiritual leaders, Survivors, schools of theology, seminaries, and other religious training centres, to develop and teach curriculum for all student clergy, and all clergy and staff who work in Aboriginal communities, on the need to respect Indigenous spirituality in its own right, the history and legacy of residential schools and the roles of the church parties in that system, the history and legacy of religious conflict in Aboriginal families and communities, and the responsibility that churches have to mitigate such conflicts and prevent spiritual violence.

61 We call upon church parties to the Settlement Agreement, in collaboration with Survivors and representatives of Aboriginal organizations, to establish permanent funding to Aboriginal people for:

i   Community-controlled healing and reconciliation projects.

ii Community-controlled culture and language revitalization projects.

iii Community-controlled education and relationship building projects.

iv Regional dialogues for Indigenous spiritual leaders and youth to discuss Indigenous spirituality, self-determination, and reconciliation.

EDUCATION FOR RECONCILIATION

62 We call upon the federal, provincial, and territorial governments, in consultation and collaboration with Survivors, Aboriginal peoples, and educators, to:

i   Make age-appropriate curriculum on residential schools, Treaties, and Aboriginal peoples' historical and contemporary contributions to Canada a mandatory education requirement for Kindergarten to Grade Twelve students.

ii Provide the necessary funding to post-secondary institutions to educate teachers on how to integrate Indigenous knowledge and teaching methods into classrooms.

iii Provide the necessary funding to Aboriginal schools to utilize Indigenous knowledge and teaching methods in classrooms.

iv Establish senior-level positions in government at the assistant deputy minister level or higher dedicated to Aboriginal content in education.

63 We call upon the Council of Ministers of Education, Canada to maintain an annual commitment to Aboriginal education issues, including:

i Developing and implementing Kindergarten to Grade Twelve curriculum and learning resources on Aboriginal peoples in Canadian history, and the history and legacy of residential schools.

ii Sharing information and best practices on teaching curriculum related to residential schools and Aboriginal history.

iii Building student capacity for intercultural understanding, empathy, and mutual respect.

iv Identifying teacher-training needs relating to the above.

64 We call upon all levels of government that provide public funds to denominational schools to require such schools to provide an education on comparative religious studies, which must include a segment on Aboriginal spiritual beliefs and practices developed in collaboration with Aboriginal Elders.

65 We call upon the federal government, through the Social Sciences and Humanities Research Council, and in collaboration with Aboriginal peoples, post-secondary institutions and educators, and the National Centre for Truth and Reconciliation and its partner institutions, to establish a national research program with multi-year funding to advance understanding of reconciliation.

YOUTH PROGRAMS

66 We call upon the federal government to establish multiyear funding for community-based youth organizations to deliver programs on reconciliation, and establish a national network to share information and best practices.

MUSEUMS AND ARCHIVES

67 We call upon the federal government to provide funding to the Canadian Museums Association to undertake, in collaboration with Aboriginal peoples, a national review of museum policies and best practices to determine the level of compliance with the *United Nations Declaration on the Rights of Indigenous Peoples* and to make recommendations.

68 We call upon the federal government, in collaboration with Aboriginal peoples, and the Canadian Museums Association to mark the 150th anniversary of Canadian Confederation in 2017 by establishing a dedicated national funding program for commemoration projects on the theme of reconciliation.

69 We call upon Library and Archives Canada to:

i   Fully adopt and implement the *United Nations Declaration on the Rights of Indigenous Peoples* and the *United Nations Joinet-Orentlicher Principles*, as related to Aboriginal peoples' inalienable right to know the truth about what happened and why, with regard to human rights violations committed against them in the residential schools.

ii   Ensure that its record holdings related to residential schools are accessible to the public.

iii Commit more resources to its public education materials and programming on residential schools.

70 We call upon the federal government to provide funding to the Canadian Association of Archivists to undertake, in collaboration with Aboriginal peoples, a national review of archival policies and best practices to:

i Determine the level of compliance with the *United Nations Declaration on the Rights of Indigenous Peoples* and the *United Nations Joinet-Orentlicher Principles*, as related to Aboriginal peoples' inalienable right to know the truth about what happened and why, with regard to human rights violations committed against them in the residential schools.

ii Produce a report with recommendations for full implementation of these international mechanisms as a reconciliation framework for Canadian archives.

MISSING CHILDREN AND BURIAL INFORMATION

71 We call upon all chief coroners and provincial vital statistics agencies that have not provided to the Truth and Reconciliation Commission of Canada their records on the deaths of Aboriginal children in the care of residential school authorities to make these documents available to the National Centre for Truth and Reconciliation.

72 We call upon the federal government to allocate sufficient resources to the National Centre for Truth and Reconciliation to allow it to develop and maintain the National Residential School Student Death Register established by the Truth and Reconciliation Commission of Canada.

73 We call upon the federal government to work with churches, Aboriginal communities, and former residential school students to establish and maintain an online registry of residential school cemeteries, including, where possible, plot maps showing the location of deceased residential school children.

74 We call upon the federal government to work with the churches and Aboriginal community leaders to inform the families of children who died at residential schools of the child's burial location, and to respond to families' wishes for appropriate commemoration ceremonies and markers, and reburial in home communities where requested.

75 We call upon the federal government to work with provincial, territorial, and municipal governments, churches, Aboriginal communities, former residential school students, and current landowners to develop and implement strategies and procedures for the ongoing identification, documentation, maintenance, commemoration, and protection of residential school cemeteries or other sites at which residential school children were buried. This is to include the provision of appropriate memorial ceremonies and commemorative markers to honour the deceased children.

76 We call upon the parties engaged in the work of documenting, maintaining, commemorating, and protecting residential school cemeteries to adopt strategies in accordance with the following principles:

i   The Aboriginal community most affected shall lead the development of such strategies.

ii Information shall be sought from residential school Survivors and other Knowledge Keepers in the development of such strategies.

iii Aboriginal protocols shall be respected before any potentially invasive technical inspection and investigation of a cemetery site.

NATIONAL CENTRE FOR TRUTH AND RECONCILIATION

77 We call upon provincial, territorial, municipal, and community archives to work collaboratively with the National Centre for Truth and Reconciliation to identify and collect copies of all records relevant to the history and legacy of the residential school system, and to provide these to the National Centre for Truth and Reconciliation.

78 We call upon the Government of Canada to commit to making a funding contribution of $10 million over seven years to the National Centre for Truth and Reconciliation, plus an additional amount to assist communities to research and produce histories of their own residential school experience and their involvement in truth, healing, and reconciliation.

COMMEMORATION

79 We call upon the federal government, in collaboration with Survivors, Aboriginal organizations, and the arts community, to develop a reconciliation framework for Canadian heritage and commemoration. This would include, but not be limited to:

i   Amending the Historic Sites and Monuments Act to
     include First Nations, Inuit, and Métis representation
     on the Historic Sites and Monuments Board of Can-
     ada and its Secretariat.

ii   Revising the policies, criteria, and practices of the
     National Program of Historical Commemoration to
     integrate Indigenous history, heritage values, and
     memory practices into Canada's national heritage and
     history.

iii Developing and implementing a national heritage
     plan and strategy for commemorating residential
     school sites, the history and legacy of residential
     schools, and the contributions of Aboriginal peoples
     to Canada's history.

80   We call upon the federal government, in collaboration
     with Aboriginal peoples, to establish, as a statutory
     holiday, a National Day for Truth and Reconciliation
     to honour Survivors, their families, and communities,
     and ensure that public commemoration of the history
     and legacy of residential schools remains a vital com-
     ponent of the reconciliation process.

81   We call upon the federal government, in collaboration
     with Survivors and their organizations, and other par-
     ties to the Settlement Agreement, to commission and
     install a publicly accessible, highly visible, Residential
     Schools National Monument in the city of Ottawa to
     honour Survivors and all the children who were lost
     to their families and communities.

82   We call upon provincial and territorial governments,
     in collaboration with Survivors and their organiza-

tions, and other parties to the Settlement Agreement, to commission and install a publicly accessible, highly visible, Residential Schools Monument in each capital city to honour Survivors and all the children who were lost to their families and communities.

83 We call upon the Canada Council for the Arts to establish, as a funding priority, a strategy for Indigenous and non-Indigenous artists to undertake collaborative projects and produce works that contribute to the reconciliation process.

MEDIA AND RECONCILIATION

84 We call upon the federal government to restore and increase funding to the CBC/Radio-Canada, to enable Canada's national public broadcaster to support reconciliation, and be properly reflective of the diverse cultures, languages, and perspectives of Aboriginal peoples, including, but not limited to:

i   Increasing Aboriginal programming, including Aboriginal-language speakers.

ii Increasing equitable access for Aboriginal peoples to jobs, leadership positions, and professional development opportunities within the organization.

iii Continuing to provide dedicated news coverage and online public information resources on issues of concern to Aboriginal peoples and all Canadians, including the history and legacy of residential schools and the reconciliation process.

85 We call upon the Aboriginal Peoples Television Network, as an independent non-profit broadcaster with programming by, for, and about Aboriginal peoples, to support reconciliation, including but not limited to:

i   Continuing to provide leadership in programming and organizational culture that reflects the diverse cultures, languages, and perspectives of Aboriginal peoples.

ii   Continuing to develop media initiatives that inform and educate the Canadian public, and connect Aboriginal and non-Aboriginal Canadians.

86 We call upon Canadian journalism programs and media schools to require education for all students on the history of Aboriginal peoples, including the history and legacy of residential schools, the *United Nations Declaration on the Rights of Indigenous Peoples*, Treaties and Aboriginal rights, Indigenous law, and Aboriginal–Crown relations.

SPORTS AND RECONCILIATION

87 We call upon all levels of government, in collaboration with Aboriginal peoples, sports halls of fame, and other relevant organizations, to provide public education that tells the national story of Aboriginal athletes in history.

88 We call upon all levels of government to take action to ensure long-term Aboriginal athlete development and growth, and continued support for the North American Indigenous Games, including funding to host the games and for provincial and territorial team preparation and travel.

89 We call upon the federal government to amend the Physical Activity and Sport Act to support reconciliation by ensuring that policies to promote physical activity as a fundamental element of health and well-being, reduce barriers to sports participation, increase the pursuit of excellence in sport, and build capacity in the Canadian sport system, are inclusive of Aboriginal peoples.

90 We call upon the federal government to ensure that national sports policies, programs, and initiatives are inclusive of Aboriginal peoples, including, but not limited to, establishing:

i   In collaboration with provincial and territorial governments, stable funding for, and access to, community sports programs that reflect the diverse cultures and traditional sporting activities of Aboriginal peoples.

ii   An elite athlete development program for Aboriginal athletes.

iii   Programs for coaches, trainers, and sports officials that are culturally relevant for Aboriginal peoples.

iv   Anti-racism awareness and training programs.

91 We call upon the officials and host countries of international sporting events such as the Olympics, Pan Am, and Commonwealth games to ensure that Indigenous peoples' territorial protocols are respected, and local Indigenous communities are engaged in all aspects of planning and participating in such events.

BUSINESS AND RECONCILIATION

92 We call upon the corporate sector in Canada to adopt the *United Nations Declaration on the Rights of Indigenous Peoples* as a reconciliation framework and to apply its principles, norms, and standards to corporate policy and core operational activities involving Indigenous peoples and their lands and resources. This would include, but not be limited to, the following:

i   Commit to meaningful consultation, building respectful relationships, and obtaining the free, prior, and informed consent of Indigenous peoples before proceeding with economic development projects.

ii   Ensure that Aboriginal peoples have equitable access to jobs, training, and education opportunities in the corporate sector, and that Aboriginal communities gain long-term sustainable benefits from economic development projects.

iii   Provide education for management and staff on the history of Aboriginal peoples, including the history and legacy of residential schools, the *United Nations Declaration on the Rights of Indigenous Peoples*, Treaties and Aboriginal rights, Indigenous law, and Aboriginal–Crown relations. This will require skills based training in intercultural competency, conflict resolution, human rights, and anti-racism.

NEWCOMERS TO CANADA

93 We call upon the federal government, in collaboration with the national Aboriginal organizations, to revise the information kit for newcomers to Canada and its citizenship test to reflect a more inclusive history of the diverse Aboriginal peoples of Canada, including information about the Treaties and the history of residential schools.

94 We call upon the Government of Canada to replace the Oath of Citizenship with the following:

I swear (or affirm) that I will be faithful and bear true allegiance to Her Majesty Queen Elizabeth II, Queen of Canada, Her Heirs and Successors, and that I will faithfully observe the laws of Canada including Treaties with Indigenous Peoples, and fulfill my duties as a Canadian citizen.

Classroom Activities, Discussion Guide, and Additional Reading

IIIIIIIIIIIIIIIIIIIIIIIIIIIIIIIIIIIIIIIIIIIIIIIIIIIIIIIIIIIIIIIIIIIIIIIIIIIIIIIIII

Personal/Professional Pledge of Reconciliation

Read and discuss the Truth and Reconciliation Commission's 94 Calls to Action (see Appendix 3).

Develop your own personal and/or professional Pledge of Reconciliation with Indigenous Peoples. Here's a sample to get you started.

Personal Pledge of Reconciliation with Indigenous Peoples

I, _____ , in the spirit of reconciliation with Indigenous Peoples in Canada, solemnly pledge:

- To learn more about Indigenous Peoples and issues.
- To continue to look forward to positive change for the situation of Indigenous Peoples.
- To find ways to address the Indigenous-related myths and misconceptions with my fellow Canadians.

- To not perpetuate stereotypes in my conversations or observations.
- To encourage others around me to keep reconciliation an ongoing effort.
- To actively encourage ongoing support of National Indigenous Peoples Day every June 21st for myself, my family, my community, and my colleagues.

Signature: _____

Date: _____

Classroom Activities

Indian Act Timeline Activity (to be done in advance of reading the book)

- Ask the group to individually write down *Indian Act* and Indigenous history dates they know on cards or pieces of paper.
- Have the students line up the cards chronologically.
- Record the dates on a flipchart.
- Fill in the blanks as the group works through the book.

Matching Exercise

Draw up a list of words and their definition, mix them up, and ask the students to connect them. Here's an example of words and definitions that you could scramble for students:

Potlatch	Cultural ceremony
Duncan Campbell Scott	Deputy Superintendent of Indian Affairs

Band elections	Imposed over traditional leadership
Bagot Report	Root of the *Indian Act*
Dr. Peter Bryce	Wrote about health of children in residential schools
Status Indian	Registered under the *Indian Act*
Permit to pass	Required so Indians could leave reserve

True or False Exercise

Please indicate which of the following 10 statements were arguments on the right-to-vote debate and which ones are made up:

1   Indians were incapable of exercising the franchise.
TRUE   FALSE

2   Indians were not capable of civilization and would eventually become extinct.
TRUE   FALSE

3   Indians were utterly incapable of managing their own affairs, and the numerous legal disabilities imposed on them by the *Indian Act* made extension of the franchise inappropriate.
TRUE   FALSE

4   There should be no representation without taxation.
TRUE   FALSE

5 The vote should not be extended to Indians involved in the 1885 rebellion.

TRUE   FALSE

6 Indian property interests in reserve lands not equivalent to non-native property interests.

TRUE   FALSE

7 Indians should not have the vote while under the discretionary care of the government.

TRUE   FALSE

8 Indians were too controlled by government and therefore interference by Indian agents was possible.

TRUE   FALSE

9 There was fear that the true intent of the bill was gerrymandering.

TRUE   FALSE

10 Extending the vote to Indians represented and encroachment on the rights of white men.

TRUE   FALSE

Answers on next page

Discussion Guide

1 Why do you think so little is known about the *Indian Act*?

2 How does knowing more about the *Indian Act* affect your life?

3 Which aspects of the *Indian Act* were most disturbing to you?

4 What do you think of the language the author used in the book? Was it passionate? Dispassionate? Objective? Inflammatory? Powerful? Weak?

5 Which aspects of the book made you feel uncomfortable? Do you feel as though the author is laying blame in any way on the non-Indigenous population?

6 How has this book affected your view of Canada's history and its founding father, John A. Macdonald? Does removing statues and renaming buildings contribute to reconciliation or erase history?

7 How does this book influence the way you now perceive Indigenous Peoples?

8 What are the social and political impacts of removing the *Indian Act* as a piece of legislature?

9 Which of the Truth and Reconciliation Commission's 94 Calls to Action were relevant to you personally? Professionally?

10 Has this book broadened your understanding of the issues faced by Indigenous Peoples today?

21 Things You Can Do to Help Change the World

1 Attend or volunteer at a National Indigenous Peoples Day event.

2 Participate in a Walk for Reconciliation or organize one.

3 Attend and support Indigenous community events.

4 Donate books by Indigenous authors to school libraries.

5 Ask your children's teachers if they include curriculum related to residential schools and the *Indian Act*.

6 Read books by Indigenous authors.

7 Read books by Indigenous authors to your children (see Reading List for suggestions).

ANSWER: If you said all 10 arguments were true, then you are right.

8   Donate sports equipment to remote Indigenous communities.

9   Donate time to coach Indigenous sports teams in your community.

10 Ensure you buy authentic Indigenous art.

11 Buy food from an Indigenous food truck; eat in an Indigenous-owned restaurant

12 Learn the Indigenous names for where you live and work.

13 Support Indigenous language revitalization.

14 Attend an Indigenous film festival.

15 Attend an Indigenous music festival.

16 Attend a pow wow.

17 Support efforts to stop inappropriate usage of Indigenous imagery for mascots.

18 Speak up when you observe cultural appropriation.* Ensure you don't promote cultural appropriation when choosing a Halloween costume

19 Speak up when you hear someone making derogatory remarks about Indigenous Peoples.

20 Write a letter to your MP to support the dismantling of the *Indian Act.*

21 Encourage family and friends to commit to helping you change the world.

---

* Cultural appropriation is defined by law professor Susan Scafaldi as "Taking intellectual property, traditional knowledge, cultural expressions, or artifacts from someone else's culture without permission. This can include unauthorized use of another culture's dance, dress, music, language, folklore, cuisine, traditional medicine, religious symbols, etc. It's most likely to be harmful when the source community is a minority group *that has been oppressed or exploited in other ways or when the object of appropriation is particularly sensitive, such as a sacred objects."* [1]

Additional Reading

Menno Boldt, *Surviving as Indians: The Challenge of Self-Government* (University of Toronto Press, 1993).

Douglas Cole and Ira Chaikin, *Iron Hand upon the People: The Law against the Potlatch on the Northwest Coast* (Douglas & McIntyre, 1990).

Calvin Helin, *Dancing with Dependency: Out of Poverty through Self-Reliance* (Ravencrest Publishing, 2008).

Robert P.C. (Bob) Joseph and Cynthia F. Joseph, *Working Effectively with Indigenous Peoples®* (Indigenous Relations Press, Port Coquitlam, Canada, 2017).

Thomas King, *The Inconvenient Indian: A Curious Account of Native People in North America* (Doubleday Canada, 2012).

Arthur Manuel and Grand Chief Ronald M. Derrickson, *Unsettling Canada: A National Wake-Up Call* (Between the Lines, 2015).

John Ralston Saul, *The Comeback* (Penguin Books, 2014).

Ronald Wright, *Stolen Continents: The "New World" through Indian Eyes* (Penguin Books, 1992).

BOOKS FOR CHILDREN AND YOUTH

Christy Jordan-Fenton and Margaret Pokiak-Fenton, *Fatty Legs: A True Story* (Annick Press, 2010).

Christy Jordan-Fenton and Margaret Pokiak-Fenton, *A Stranger at Home: A True Story*, artwork by Liz Amini-Holmes (Annick Press, 2011).

Sylvia Olsen with Rita Morris and Ann Sam, *No Time to Say Goodbye: Children's Stories of Kuper Island Residential School* (Sono Nis Press, 2003).

David A. Robertson, *7 Generations: A Plains Cree Saga* (Highwater Press, A Division of Portage & Main Press, 2010).

Quotes from Sir John A. Macdonald and Duncan Campbell Scott

||||||||||||||||||||||||||||||||||||||||||||||||||||||||||||||||||||||||||||||||||||||||||||||||||||

WE HAVE COLLECTED a few statements from both these men, and one letter, from Prime Minister John A. Macdonald, relating to Indigenous Peoples. In our research we found a great many sites with quotes by Macdonald, as he was considered a great orator, but the lists of quotes did not contain any of the following:

"When the school is on the reserve, the child lives with its parents, who are savages, and though he may learn to read and write, his habits and training mode of thought are Indian. He is simply a savage who can read and write. It has been strongly impressed upon myself, as head of the Department, that Indian children should be withdrawn as much as possible from the parental influence, and the only way to do that would be to put them in central training industrial schools where they will acquire the habits and modes of thought of white men." *1879*

"It is worthy of consideration whether legislative measures should not be adopted for the establishment of some kind of municipal system among such bands as are found sufficiently advanced to justify the experiment being tried. It is hoped that a system may be adopted which will have the effect of accustoming the Indians to the modes of government prevalent in the white communities surrounding them, and that it will thus tend to prepare them for earlier amalgamation with the general population of the country." *1880*

"... we have been pampering and coaxing the Indians; that we must take a new course, we must vindicate the position of the white man, we must teach the Indians what law is; we must not pauperise them, as they say we have been doing." *1885*

"We have done all we could to put them on themselves; we have done all we could to make them work as agriculturists; we have done all we could, by the supply of cattle, agricultural implements and instruction, to change them from a nomadic to an agricultural life. We have had very considerable success; we have had infinitely more success during our short period, than the United States have had during twenty-five years. We have had a wonderful success; but still we have had the Indians; and then in these half-breeds, enticed by white men, the savage instinct was awakened; the desire of plunder—aye, and, perhaps, the desire of scalping—the savage idea of a warlike glory, which pervades the breast of most men, civilised or uncivilised, was aroused in them, and forgetting all the kindness that had been bestowed upon them, forgetting all the gifts that had been given to them, forgetting all that the Government, the white people and the Parliament of Canada had been doing for them, in trying to rescue them from barbarity; forgetting that we had given them reserves, the means to cultivate those reserves, and the means of education how to cultivate them—forgetting all these things, they rose against us." *1885*

"We acquired the North-West country in 1870. Not a life was lost, not a blow was struck, not a pound nor a dollar was spent in warfare, in that long period that has since intervened. I have not hesitated to tell this House, again and again, that we could not always hope to maintain peace with the Indians; that the savage was still a savage, and that until he ceased to be savage, we were always in danger of a collision, in danger of war, in danger of an outbreak. I am only surprised that we have been able so long to maintain peace—that from 1870 until 1885 not one single blow, not one single murder, not one single loss of life, has taken place." *1885*

"He shall die though every dog in Québec bark in his favour." *1885, following execution of Louis Riel for treason*

"The great aim of our legislation has been to do away with the tribal system and assimilate the Indian people in all respects with the other inhabitants of the Dominion as speedily as they are fit to change." *1887*

"The third clause provides that celebrating the 'Potlatch' is a misdemeanour. This Indian festival is debauchery of the worst kind, and the departmental officers and all clergymen unite in affirming that it is absolutely necessary to put this practice down." *1894*

HERE ARE SOME quotes from Duncan Campbell Scott. Scott who, as Deputy Superintendent General of Indian Affairs from 1913 until 1932, took the groundwork of Macdonald's legacy of repressive policies towards Indigenous Peoples further down the continuum of assimilation.

"The purpose of the Amendment to the Act was to prevent the Indians from being exploited as a savage or semi-savage race, when the whole of the administrative force of the Department is endeavouring to civilize them." *1916*

"It has always been clear to me that the Indians must have some sort of recreation, and if our agents would endeavour to substitute reasonable amusements for this senseless drumming and dancing, it would be a great assistance." *1921*

"It is the opinion of the writer that ... the Government will in time reach the end of its responsibility as the Indians progress into civilization and finally disappear as a separate and distinct people, not by race extinction but by gradual assimilation with their fellow-citizens." *1931*

"One can hardly be sympathetic with the contemporary Sundance or Potlatch when one knows that the original spirit has departed and that they are largely the opportunities for debauchery by low white men." *1941*

Notes

IIIIIIIIIIIIIIIIIIIIIIIIII

THE INDIAN ACT

1 Canada, Department of the Interior, *Annual Report for the Year Ended 30th June, 1876, Sessional Papers*, 1877, vol. 7, no. 11, xiv.

2 Scott Papers, Library and Archives of Canada, R.G. 10, vol. 6810, file 473, vol. 12, Hearings Testimony, 1921–22.

3 Canada, "A New Future" (Canadian residential school propaganda video), 1955, https://www.youtube.com/watch?v=s_v4d7sXoqU.

4 Union of BC Indian Chiefs, Indian Government Portfolio, *Aboriginal Rights Position Paper Resource Kit* (Vancouver: Union of BC Indian Chiefs, 1979), 129.

5 For more information on the often overlooked villainous nature of the Royal Proclamation, please read Menno Boldt's *Surviving as Indians: The Challenge of Self-Government* (University of Toronto Press, 1993), Chapter 1: "Justice."

CHAPTER 1

1 Sir John A. Macdonald, in Canada, *House of Commons Debates*, 8th Parliament, 1st Session, 5 May 1880.

2 *An Act to Amend the Act Providing for the Organization of the Department of the Secretary of the State of Canada*, S.C. 1876, c. 6.

3 Proceedings, Atlantic Policy Congress of First Nations Chiefs Secretariat, October 27, 2009, Lawrence Paul, co-chair, quoted in Standing Senate Committee on Aboriginal Peoples, *First Nations Elections: The Choice Is Inherently Theirs: Report of the Standing Senate Committee on Aboriginal Peoples* (Ottawa, 2010), 27.

4 Deputy Superintendent William Spragge to Secretary of State Joseph Howe, *Report of the Indian Branch of the Department of the Secretary of State for the Provinces, 1870, Sessional Papers*, 1871.

5   Ibid.

6   *Indian Act, 1876*, S.C. 1876, s. 63.

7   *An Act for the Gradual Enfranchisement of Indians, the Better
    Management of Indian Affairs, and to Extend the Provisions of the Act
    31st Victoria*, S.C. 1870, c. 42.

8   In Cora Woolsey, "The Indian Act: The Social Engineering of
    Canada's First Nations," *vis-à-vis: Explorations in Anthropology* 12,
    no. 1 (2013): 20–30, http://vav.library.utoronto.ca/index.php/vav/
    article/view/15110/17126.

9   Peggy J. Blair, *Fact Sheet: Rights of Aboriginal Women On- and Off-
    Reserve* (Scow Institute, 2005), 1.

10 *Canadian Charter of Rights and Freedoms, Part I of the Constitution Act,
    1982, being Schedule B to the Canada Act 1982* (UK), 1982, c. 11.

11 Royal Commission on Aboriginal Peoples, *Report of the Royal
    Commission on Aboriginal Peoples*, vol. 4: *Perspectives and Realities*
    (Ottawa: Minister of Supply and Services Canada, 1996), 35.

12 Native Women's Association of Canada, *Fact Sheet: Missing and
    Murdered Aboriginal Women and Girls in Ontario* (Ottawa: Native
    Women's Association of Canada, 2010), 2.

13 Blair, *Fact Sheet: Rights of Aboriginal Women On- and Off-Reserve*, 3.

14 Prime Minister John A. Macdonald to Adams George Archibald,
    Lieutenant-Governor of Manitoba, 18 November 1870.

15 Royal Commission on Aboriginal Peoples, *Report of the Royal
    Commission on Aboriginal Peoples*, vol. 2: *Restructuring the Relationship*
    (Ottawa: Minister of Supply and Services Canada, 1996), 429.

16 Library and Archives of Canada, R.G. 10 (Indian Affairs), vol. 245,
    part 2, no. 11801-11900, microfilm reel C12339, in Royal Commission
    on Aboriginal Peoples, *Report of the Royal Commission on Aboriginal
    Peoples*, vol. 1: *Looking Forward, Looking Back* (Ottawa: Minister of
    Supply and Services Canada, 1996), 137.

17 *Indian Act, 1880*, S.C. 1880, c. 28, *An Act to Amend and Consolidate
    the Laws Respecting Indians*, s. 99.

CHAPTER 2

1   Canada, *House of Common Debates*, 5th Parliament, 3rd Session (6
    June 1885–20 July 1885) (Ottawa: Maclean, Roger & Co., 1885),
    3110–3119.

2   Thomas King, *The Inconvenient Indian: A Curious Account of Native
    People in North America* (Toronto: Doubleday Canada, 2012), 227–228.

3   *Indian Act, 1876*, S.C. 1876, c. 81.

4   *Indian Act, 1886*, S.C. 1886, c. 28.
5   Arthur J. Ray, *An Illustrated History of Canada's Native People*, 4th edition (Montreal: McGill-Queen's University Press, 2016), 260.
6   Timeline based on Mapping Tool: Kitsilano Reserve, http://indigenousfoundations.arts.ubc.ca/mapping_tool_kitsilano_reserve/.
7   Indigenous and Northern Affairs Canada, "The Indian Register" (January 2011), https://www.aadnc- aandc.gc.ca/eng/1100100032475/1100100032476.
8   Bob Joseph and Cynthia F. Joseph, *Working Effectively with Indigenous Peoples®* (Port Coquitlam, BC: Indigenous Relations Press, 2017), 31.
9   Regulations, Protection of Indian Reserves, S.G.I.A. [Superintendent General of Indian Affairs], Order-in-Council 1888-1791, approved 9 August 1888, R.G. 2, Privy Council Office, Series A-1-a.
10 Rebecca Bateman, "Talking with the Plow: Agricultural Policy and Indian Farming in the Canadian and US Prairies," *Canadian Journal of Native Studies* 16, no. 2 (1996): 219.

CHAPTER 3

1   R. Douglas Francis et al., *Destinies: Canadian History since Confederation* (Toronto: Nelson Publishing, 2008), 44.
2   *An Act to Further Amend the Indian Act, 1880*, S.C. 1882, c. 27 (2).
3   *The Indian Advancement Act, 1884*, S.C. 1884, c. 28.
4   Royal Commission on Aboriginal Peoples, *Report*, vol. 1: *Looking Forward, Looking Back*, 550.
5   *Regina Leader-Post*, 18 May 1961.
6   Christine Sismondo and Simon Beggs, "Firewater," *The Walrus* 7, no. 6 (July/August 2010).
7   Judge Alfred Scow, Royal Commission of Aboriginal Peoples, *Transcriptions of Public Hearings and Round Table Discussions, 1992–1993*, Ottawa, 26 November 1992, 344–345.
8   Duncan Campbell Scott to W.M. Graham, 4 October 1921, in Brian Titley, *A Narrow Vision: Duncan Campbell Scott and the Administration of Indian Affairs in Canada* (Vancouver: UBC Press, 1986), 177.
9   Hayter Reed to Edgar Dewdney, 20 July 1885, Library and Archives of Canada, R.G. 10, vol. 3710, file 19, 550-3.
10 F.L. Barron, "The Indian Pass System in the Canadian West, 1882–1935," *Prairie Forum* 13, no. 1 (Spring 1988): 34–35.
11 *Indian Act, 1884*, S.C. 1884, c. 32, s. 11.
12 Truth and Reconciliation Commission of Canada, *Historical Overview*, http://www.trc.ca/websites/trcinstitution/index.php?p=39.

13 National Centre for Truth and Reconciliation, *A Knock on the Door: The Essential History of Residential Schools from the Truth and Reconciliation Commission of Canada* (Winnipeg: University of Manitoba Press, 2016), 209.

14 James Waldram and D. Ann Herring, *Aboriginal Health in Canada: Historical, Cultural, and Epidemiological Perspectives* (Toronto: University of Toronto Press, 2006), 167.

15 Canada, *House of Commons Debates*, 5th Parliament, 1st Session, 1107–1108 (9 May 1883).

16 *Indian Act, 1927*, R.S.C. 1927, c. 98, *An Act Respecting Indians*.

17 *Saturday Night Magazine*, 23 November 1907.

18 Superintendent D.C. Scott to Indian Agent General Major D. McKay, 12 April 1910, Library and Archives of Canada, Department of Indian Affairs, R.G. 1

19 P.H. Bryce, *Being the Story of a National Crime: An Appeal for Justice to the Indians of Canada, the Wards of the Nation, Our Allies in the Revolutionary War, Our Brothers-in-Arms in the Great War* (James Hope & Sons Limited, 1922), 6.

20 Sean Fine, "Chief Justice Says Canada Attempted 'Cultural Genocide' on Aboriginals," *Globe and Mail*, 28 May 2015.

21 Suzanne Fournier and Ernie Crey, *Stolen from Our Embrace: The Abduction of First Nations Children and the Restoration of Aboriginal Communities* (Vancouver: Douglas & McIntyre, 1998), cited in National Collaborating Centre for Aboriginal Health, *Culture and Language as Social Determinants of First Nations, Inuit and Métis Health* (Prince George, BC: National Collaborating Centre for Aboriginal Health), 2.

22 National Collaborating Centre for Aboriginal Health, *Culture and Language as Social Determinants of First Nations, Inuit and Métis Health*, 2.

CHAPTER 4

1 Canada, *Official Report of the Debates*, House of Commons, 5th Parliament, 3rd Session (1885), vol. 20, 3119.

2 Ibid.

3 Royal Commission on Aboriginal Peoples, *Report*, vol. 1: *Looking Forward, Looking Back*, 316.

4 Truth and Reconciliation Commission of Canada, *A Knock on the Door*, 64.

5 *Indian Act, 1906*, R.S. 1906, c. 81.

6   Quoted in Roger G. Moore, John Leslie, and Ron Maguire,
    Historical Development of the Indian Act (Ottawa Treaties and
    Historical Research Centre, P.R.E. Group: Indian and Northern
    Affairs, 1978), 113.

7   Ray, *An Illustrated History of Canada's Native People*, 260.

8   Sarah Carter, "'An Infamous Proposal': Prairie Indian Reserve Land
    and Soldier Settlement after World War I, *Manitoba History*, no. 37,
    (Spring/Summer 1999), http://www.mhs.mb.ca/docs/mb_history/37/
    infamousproposal.shtml.

9   J. D. MacLean, Assistant Deputy and Secretary to E. S. Gauthier,
    Indian agent, 30 August 1922.

10 King, *The Inconvenient Indian*, 155.

11 *Indian Act, 1927*, R.S. 1927, c. 98.

12 Chief Joe Mathias and Gary R. Yabsley, "Conspiracy of Legislation:
    The Suppression of Indian Rights in Canada," *BC Studies*, no. 89
    (Spring 1991).

13 *An Act to Amend the Indian Act*, S.C. 1926–27, c. 32, s. 2; *An Act to
    Amend the Indian Act*, S.C. 1930, c. 25, s. 16.

14 *Indian Act*, R.S.C., 1985, c. 1–5.

CHAPTER 5

1   Duncan Campbell Scott, *The Administration of Indian Affairs in
    Canada* (Toronto, 1931), 27.

2   Truth and Reconciliation Commission of Canada, *Final Report of
    the Truth and Reconciliation Commission of Canada*, vol. I: *Canada's
    Residential Schools: The History, Part 2, 1939 to 2000* (Montreal:
    McGill-Queen's Native and Northern Series, 2016), 36.

3   Truth and Reconciliation Commission of Canada, *Final Report of
    the Truth and Reconciliation Commission of Canada*, vol. 1: *Summary:
    Honouring the Truth, Reconciling for the Future* (Toronto: James
    Lorimer, 2015), 154.

4   Wendy Moss and Elaine Gardner-O'Toole, *Aboriginal People: History
    of Discriminatory Laws* (Ottawa: Library of Parliament Research
    Branch, 1987, revised 1991).

5   *Royal Proclamation 1763, Given at our Court at St. James's the 7th Day
    of October 1763 in the Third Year of our Reign.*

6   Stephen Harper, 2009 Group of Twenty (G20) meeting, Pittsburgh,
    Pennsylvania.

7   Harold Cardinal, *The Unjust Society: The Tragedy of Canada's Indians*,
    2nd ed. (Vancouver: Douglas & McIntyre, 1969), 140.

8   Canada, Department of Indian Affairs and Northern Development, *Statement of the Government of Canada on Indian Policy* (The White Paper) (Ottawa, 1969).

CHAPTER 6

1   Ovide Mercredi and Mary Ellen Turpel, *In the Rapids: Navigating the Future of First Nations* (Toronto: Viking, 1993).
2   Royal Commission on Aboriginal Peoples, *Report of the Royal Commission on Aboriginal Peoples*, vol. 5: *Renewal: A Twenty-Year Commitment* (Ottawa: Minister of Supply and Services Canada, 1996), 1.
3   Canada, *Federal Policy Guide: Aboriginal Self-Government—The Government of Canada's Approach to Implementation of the Inherent Right and the Negotiation of Aboriginal Self-Government*, 1995, Part 1: "Policy Framework: The Inherent Right of Self-Government Is a Section 35 Right," https://www.aadnc-aandc.gc.ca/eng/1100100031843/1100100031844.
4   Ibid.
5   Lynn Brooks, Executive Director, Status of Women Council of the Northwest Territories, Yellowknife, Northwest Territories, Testimony before the Royal Commission on Aboriginal Peoples, 7 December 1992, in Canada, *Royal Commission on Aboriginal Peoples, Report*, vol. 4: *Perspectives and Realities*, 70.
6   Canada, Department of Justice, "Principles Respecting the Government of Canada's Relationship with Indigenous Peoples," 4 October 2017, http://www.justice.gc.ca/eng/csj-sjc/principles-principes.html.

CHAPTER 7

1   Prime Minister's Office, "New Ministers to Support the Renewed Relationship with Indigenous Peoples" (press release), Ottawa, 28 August 2017, http://pm.gc.ca/eng/news/2017/08/28/new-ministers-support-renewed-relationship-indigenous-peoples.

APPENDIX 4

1   Susan Scafidi, quoted in Nadra Kareem Nittle, "What Is Cultural Appropriation? When Is It Wrong to 'Borrow' from Another Culture?" *ThoughtCo*, 11 October 2017, https://www.thoughtco.com/cultural-appropriation-and-why-its-wrong-2834561.

Index

||||||||||||||||||||||

About the Author

‖‖

Bob Joseph, founder of Indigenous Corporate Training Inc., has provided training on Indigenous relations since 1994. As a certified Master Trainer, Bob has assisted both individuals and organizations in building Indigenous relations. His Canadian clients include all levels of government, Fortune 500 companies, financial institutions, including the World Bank, small and medium corporate enterprises, and Indigenous Peoples. He has worked internationally for clients in the United States, Guatemala, Peru, and New Caledonia in the South Pacific. In 2006, Bob co-facilitated a worldwide Indigenous Peoples' round table in Switzerland, which included participants from the United Nations, Australia, New Zealand, North, Central and South America, Africa, and the Philippines.

In May 2001, Bob was profiled in an annual feature called "Training: the New Guard 2001" by the American Society of Training and Development (ASTD) in their prestigious magazine, $T + D$. Bob was one of nine trainers selected for the feature from over 70,000 members who from more than 100 countries and 15,000 organizations.

Bob additionally has worked as an associate professor at Royal Roads University. He has an educational background in business administration and international trade.

As an author and co-author, Bob has contributed to a number of resources relating to working with Indigenous Peoples. He also manages a blog called Working Effectively with Indigenous Peoples®, which is a resource that supports people in their Indigenous relations endeavours.

Bob Joseph is an Indigenous person, or more specifically, a status Indian, and is a member of the Gwawaenuk Nation. The Gwawaenuk is one of the many Kwakwaka'wakw tribes located between Comox and Port Hardy on Vancouver Island and the adjacent mainland of British Columbia. He comes from a proud potlatch family and is an initiated member of the Hamatsa Society. As the son of a hereditary chief, he will one day, in accordance with strict cultural laws, become a hereditary chief.

ABOUT INDIGENOUS CORPORATE TRAINING INC.

"Bob talks fast and provides an insight in every breath. Make sure you come with an empty mind because it will be full when you're done." C.H.

Indigenous Corporate Training Inc. (ICT) is a global training company committed to working collaboratively with regional, national, and international clients to provide a broad range of performance improvement training services geared specifically at helping individuals and organizations work effectively with Indigenous Peoples. We at ICT recognize that organizations and their shareholders are interested in demonstrated results of how performance improvement consulting expenditures contribute to the effectiveness of an organization. We go to great lengths to ensure there is a demonstrated link between performance improvement consulting measures and increased organizational effectiveness. ICT knows that funds spent on performance improvement training are at the expense of other initiatives, and we understand that the performance improvement must be the main driver of the work we do.

Our Working Effectively with Indigenous Peoples® training has been delivered to Fortune 500 companies, financial institutions, including the World Bank, small and medium corporate enterprises, and through all levels of governments across Canada. It has also been delivered in North and South America, and Switzerland.

ICT provides public, on-site, and virtual training. Our schedule for public and virtual training sessions is posted on www.ictinc.ca. To arrange for on-site training, please contact our office at info@ictinc.ca.

If you would like additional information and opportunities to learn and share ideas with others, subscribe to our free, monthly newsletter. In the newsletter you will find a variety of information to enhance your understanding of Working Effectively with Indigenous Peoples®. The newsletter can be accessed at www.ictinc.ca/newsletter-sign-up.